Contents

Recipes

About Thai Cuisine

Thai cuisine is light, fresh and traditionally seasoned with chile peppers and aromatic herbs, a gourmet delight for those who know and love good food. It has a temper. It can be as spicy hot (but not as heavy) as fiery Indian food or as gently flavored as Chinese. Happily, Thai cuisine is a pleasant contrast between the two. You can have it "spicy hot or spicy not." You decide.

The secret of Thai cooking is to maintain a delicate balance between the spices and main ingredients so that one does not overwhelm the other. Perfection comes with practice, and tasting; tasting is the key to success. Texture and color contrast is also important. These recipes will show you how.

Thai cuisine is amazingly versatile. One dish can have as many as seven or more variations. Although beef, chicken, pork and seafood are most often used, vegetarian dishes are equally popular. What a fine challenge for creative cooks.

Thai seasonings may seem complex. They're not. Many are your everyday favorites . . . garlic, onion, basil, coriander, ginger, mint, chile peppers, curry . . . plus Thai's own lemongrass, eggplant, kaffir lime leaves . . . It's the blend, the balance, that counts . . . the magic that turns American fried chicken to Thai fried chicken. Exotic! Sophisticated! Delicious! It's all here!

And now to the kitchen.

Commonly Used Ingredients

bamboo shoots

These are the edible shoots of certain bamboo plants. They are occasionally found fresh, as pictured, but are more widely available in cans. They come in many varieties and sizes. Store leftover shoots in the refrigerator, in water that is changed daily. They keep this way for about two weeks.

bananas

There are about ten different varieties of bananas in Asia: apple, cooking, egg, Chinese, lady's finger, sweet, long, seeds, etc. They all come in different sizes, shapes, colors and flavors. The most commonly used in Thai desserts are egg and apple bananas.

basil, sweet

There are many varieties of basil. The most common are sweet basil, hot basil and lemon basil. Sweet basil has a flavor similar to anise. The hot and lemon basil have flavors closer to mint. Hot basil is stronger in flavor and is very popular for stir-frying with meat among the Thais, but is not as commonly used by foreigners. Lemon basil is very popular in Laos and is used with dill in fish or chicken dishes.

bean sauce

There are many new kinds of bean sauces. The most common ones are yellow, black and red bean sauce. Thai bean sauce is usually saltier than the Chinese or Japanese versions. In addition to beans the main ingredients are salt and sugar. Most bean sauces are fermented.

bean threads

Also commonly referred to as long rice, fun see and cellophane noodles. These are fine dried noodles made from mung bean flour and sold in packets. They should be soaked for 15 to 30 minutes in warm water before using in a recipe. They have a transparent look after being soaked.

Chinese five-spice powder

This seasoning is a combination of ground fennel, star anise, ginger, licorice root, cinnamon and cloves.

Chinese parsley

Chinese parsley is also called coriander or cilantro. The leaves, roots and seeds are used in Thai cooking. Each part has a unique flavor characteristic and use. The leaves are usually used for garnishing sauces, soups and salads. The roots are simmered in clear soup broths and used in fried chicken and meat by mixing with garlic, black pepper and salt. Only Thai cooking seems to use the seeds. They have a very strong taste and are usually found in curry pastes. The Thai name is pak-chee. It is the most widely used in Thai cooking. Chinese parsley is easy to grow. There is no substitute for flavor, but if used for garnish only, then parsley can be substituted.

chile peppers

Chile peppers vary. The hottest are the very small chiles and the larger the milder. Mature chiles are not always red. The seeds are the hottest part of the chile. What makes them "hot" is capsaicin concentrated in the seeds and the inside membranes. In preparing chile paste, milder dried whole chile is sometimes called for in recipes. Dried chile must be soaked in warm water for 5 minutes, then drained. Discard the seeds. All immature peppers are green, but some mature green chile peppers never get red. If left on the plant they will turn yellow or red. Dried and powdered hot chile peppers produce cayenne. Milder red peppers are ground to produce paprika.

coconut

Coconut milk is made by grating the flesh of a fresh coconut, then pouring warm water over it. The liquid extracted when this mixture is squeezed through a cloth is the coconut milk, also available canned. Coconut milk gives body to sauces and gravies. It thickens when heated and has a sweet fragrance. It is a necessary ingredient in Thai curry dishes. Fresh coconuts contain coconut water, a popular chilled drink in Thailand.

corn, miniature

Small baby corn is available canned. An attractive addition to many dishes that need little or no cooking.

dill

Dill is an annual of the parsley family, a medium-sized herb with small feathery leaves and yellow flowers. Dill leaves can be chopped finely, fresh or dried, and sprinkled on soups, salads and seafoods. Sprigs of dill are used in red chile fish and red curries. It has a clean odor faintly reminiscent of caraway, pungent and pleasantly aromatic.

eggplant, Japanese

The long eggplant, sometimes called Japanese eggplant, is best used for stir-fry dishes.

eggplant, Thai

Sometimes served raw with a shrimp paste dip or cooked in a curry, they range from the size and shape of a pea to a cucumber or grapefruit. The pea-size eggplants are used exclusively in Laos and Thailand. All varieties differ in color and size. They come in white, green, purple, yellow or mixed colors. White or yellow eggplants are popular among the Vietnamese and Laotians and are widely used in making pickles. Pea-size eggplants are bitter and are used mainly in sauces or in green curry dishes. Green peas can be substituted for these eggplants and would appeal more to Western taste.

eryngium foetidum

The leaves of eryngium foetidum are used in salads and fish dishes. Vietnamese use them in their "Pho" (noodle soup) as a garnish.

fish sauce

This thin, translucent, salty brown sauce is an indispensable flavoring in Thai and Vietnamese cooking. It is made by salting down small fish that are packed in wooden barrels. The liquid that "runs off" is collected, cooked and bottled as fish sauce. The Vietnamese type is darker and generally more pungent than the Thai. Though the odor is strong when uncooked, the flavor mellows upon cooking. Fish sauce is milder in flavor than soy sauce and is often used in place of salt.

jackfruit

This very sweet tropical fruit is grown mainly in Southeast Asia and South America, but also in Hawaii. It grows on tree trunks and can reach the size of a watermelon.

ginger, common

Also known as green ginger, it looks like a light, brown-skinned gnarled root. When the thin skin is removed the flesh is sliced, shredded, chopped or grated. This ginger has a peppery, somewhat sweet flavor. Young ginger roots are plump, pale yellow and pink. They are often pickled, crystallized or made into a drink. Older ginger is more fibrous and much spicier and is obtainable year-round.

ginger, Thai (kha, also known as laos)

This ginger is hard in texture. It has a lighter flesh and a slightly different flavor than common ginger. Northern Thais mix it in salads. Available in dried slides and as a powder. Sometimes called ganagal. Fresh common ginger can be substituted for kha.

ginger, lesser (Kra-chai)

The tubers of this ginger look like a bunch of brownish-yellow fingers. Often added to fish curries or peeled and served as a raw vegetable.

kaffir lime leaves

Thais use a great deal of kaffir lime and its leaves…in hot-and-sour lemongrass soup, curry pastes, satay sauces and in stir-fried dishes. Fresh kaffir lime and leaves are not available in many markets. Kaffir lime has been grown successfully in the Hawaiian Islands and is available in Honolulu at the Asian Grocery. Kaffir lime does not bear fruit until it is eight to ten years old. Grated zest of fresh lime can be used as a substitute in recipes calling for grated zest of kaffir limes. Kaffir lime leaves are used for flavor, like bay leaves. They should be removed from the dish before serving.

lemongrass

Lemongrass is also called citronella and has a distinctive lemony flavor. The usual preparation method is to crush the lower part of the stalk and finely chop. Finely shredded lemon peel can be used as a substitute. The zest of $1/2$ lemon can be substituted for a stalk of lemongrass.

mint

Thais use mint leaves in their salads, stir-fried dishes and for garnishing. There are many different varieties of mint. If fresh mint is not available, simply omit it. Dried mint is not a good substitute.

mangoes

Mangoes are big business in Thailand in both the export and domestic markets. They come in many varieties, sizes, colors and tastes—from fresh green and fresh ripe to pickled, dried and canned. Fresh mangoes are sold in Thailand movie lobbies, at open markets, in specialty stores and in restaurants. As a snack they are eaten with the skin on and dripped with a fish sauce mixed with roasted ground rice, sugar, chiles and sometimes shrimp paste. Late spring through summer in Asia is definitely "mango time."

mushrooms, dried—Chinese black

The flavor of these dried mushrooms is distinctive. Sizes range from less than 1 inch to about 2 inches in diameter. They keep indefinitely when stored in tightly covered containers. Before using they must be soaked in warm water for 15 to 30 minutes. The best should be reserved for dishes in which the mushrooms are cooked whole. Less expensive mushrooms are perfect for recipes calling for slicing or quartering. Fresh mushrooms can be substituted, but are not as flavorful.

mushrooms, straw

These are thin, leaflike mushrooms available fresh or canned. They have a wonderful texture and should be used as soon as possible after the can is opened. An attractive addition to many dishes, they need little or no cooking. If not available, use small, fresh mushrooms.

noodles, rice

There are a variety of sizes. Those made from sticky rice are sometimes referred to as rice sticks. Very fine strands made from long grain rice are often called rice vermicelli noodles. Before using in a dish, rice noodles are usually presoaked in warm water. For a crisp garnish or appetizer fry noodles a small amount at a time in hot oil. They puff up and whiten instantly.

ong choi

The Thai name for this vegetable is pak-boong. This green, smooth-leafed vegetable has a flavor milder than spinach and a texture similar to watercress.

oyster sauce

A thickened brown sauce of oyster juices and salt, used both as a flavoring and a condiment. Usually, the more expensive the sauce, the better the quality. It can be stored for a long time in the refrigerator.

palm sugar

A coarse brown sugar, sold in lumps or cakes. It is made from the sap of the palmyra palm, and is used as a sweetener. Dark brown sugar can be substituted.

papaya, Thai

Papayas come in many varieties in Thailand and range in size and shape from about 5 inches to 30 inches in length. The green papaya is popular in Northeastern Thailand and Laos. Thai green papaya salad comes mixed with long string beans and anchovy; dried shrimp powder, sugar and ground peanuts; raw pickled crabs and anchovy. Some use plain papaya with tomatoes, garlic, lime juice and fish sauce. The ripe papaya is commonly served chilled as a dessert.

radish, pickled salted

Fresh white radish is sun dried, then salted and stored about one month before use. No refrigeration is required for the dark brown pickled radish. Use sparingly because it is very salty.

rice, brown

This is rice that has been hulled but has not lost its brown color. Brown rice contains more nutrients than polished white rice.

rice, sweet

A short-grain rice, quite sticky when cooked. Also called glutinous rice or sticky rice. Used in a number of thai dessert recipes.

rice flour

This is rice ground to a very fine powder. Often used as a coating before ingredients are deep fried.

rice papers

These round, paper-thin wrappers are made primarily from sticky rice. After being formed, the rice papers are dried. Dampen with water before use to make them pliable and ready for filling.

shallots

Shallots are a small, brown-skinned member of the onion family. These slender, pear-shaped bulbs are intense in taste without being unduly pungent. They grow singly or in clusters and are more seasonal than onions. Shallots taste sweet and delicate, and they are mostly used for flavoring. When recipes specify shallots, they should be used. Browning makes shallots taste a little bitter. The white part of the scallion is an acceptable substitute.

Sriracha sauce

This Thai-style pepper sauce is made from chile peppers, salt, sugar and vinegar. Not only hot and sour, but also sweet. Available in bottles in most Asian markets.

tamarind

Tamarind comes in green, ripe, dried, preserved, canned or liquid form. It has an acidic taste with a little sweet-and-sour flavor. Both the pulp and young tiny leaves are edible. Dried tamarind pulp can be soaked in warm water for 10 minutes. Squeeze the pulp into the water, then strain. Use the water in recipes. The longer the tamarind soaks, the stronger the flavor of the liquid.

tofu

Tofu is a soft white cake of pressed soybean curd. It is bland in taste, but absorbs the flavor and aroma of ingredients with which it is mixed. Considered the finest known source of low-cost, high-quality protein. It is low in saturated fats and calories and totally free of cholesterol. If not used right away, store in the refrigerator in water that is changed daily. Will keep for about five days. Tofu is also available pressed, deep fried and in dried sheets.

shrimp paste

Thick paste with greyish color and a very strong odor. If kept stored in a tightly closed jar in the refrigerator, it keeps indefinitely. Anchovy paste may be substituted.

soy sauce

Made from soybeans, flour, salt and water. Light soy sauces are lighter in color and thinner in consistency and are saltier than dark soy sauces. Dark soy sauce, or black soy sauce as they are often labeled, are sweetened with molasses. They are occasionally labeled "double dark" to indicate deeper color and strength. Use light soys for shrimp, chicken and pork; darker soys with red meats, for roasting, or for richer color in sauces. If too salty, dilute with water.

If you have difficulty in finding any of these ingredients in your local markets, please write or call:

Asian Grocery
1319 South Beretania Street
Honolulu, Hawaii 96814
Telephone (808) 531-8371 or
              (808) 536-7440

Utensils

1. Bamboo Steamer Basket
2. Aluminum Steamer for Sticky Rice
3. Stockpot
4. Aluminum Steamed Rice Server
5. Clay Mortar
6. Wooden Pestle
7. Bamboo Basket Sticky Rice Server
8. Three-Tiered Aluminum Steamer
9. Soup Server (with center section for hot charcoal)
10. Sauce Pot
11. Cleaver

Woks are used in China and throughout Southeast Asia. The unique shape of the wok allows for rapid stir-frying. This cooking method uses tossing motions when cooking in a small amount of oil over high heat to seal in flavors.

Woks are made from many different materials, the best being thin cast iron that gives very even heat. Cast-iron woks should be seasoned well before using for the first time or reseasoned if they have to be scoured to remove rust or food. Rinse the wok and dry well. Rub with oil and heat to a high temperature; cool. Repeat this process until a shiny smooth glaze has formed on the inside of the wok. From this time on all you need to do is wipe it out, rinse if necessary, dry well and return to heat to evaporate any moisture that may still be left.

Appetizers

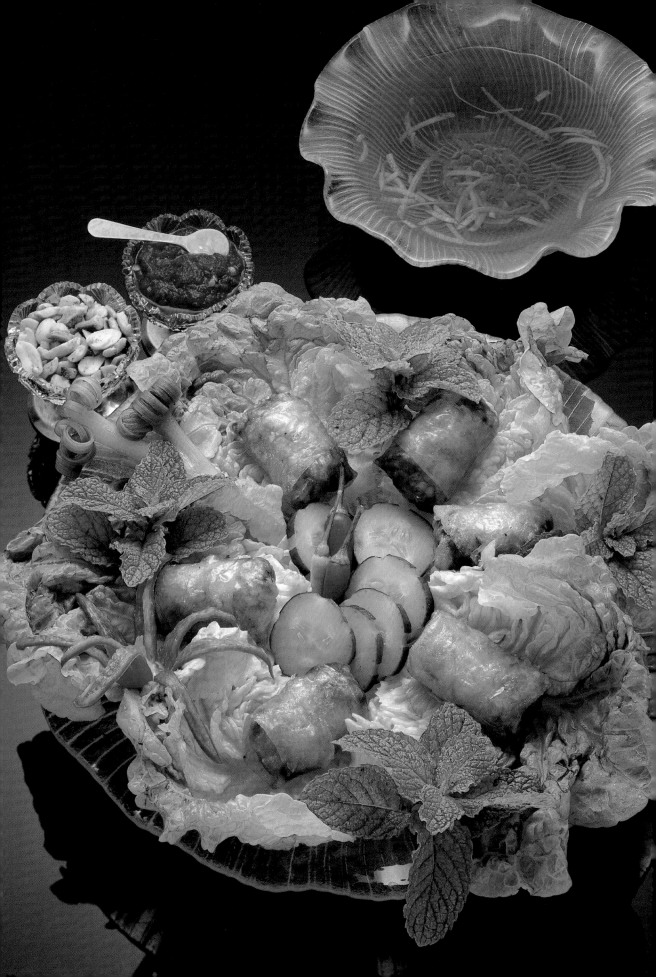

Keo's Thai Spring Rolls

ILLUSTRATED ON OPPOSITE PAGE

A highly recommended appetizer at all of Keo's restaurants. These small delicacies of pork, shrimp, mushrooms, long rice and spices are wrapped in crispy rice paper and served with fresh lettuce and mint leaves. Take the lettuce leaf, add some mint, a slice of cucumber, a spring roll and a dollop of sauce. Two to three bites and you have an excellent Thai experience.

$1/2$ pound fresh ground pork

$1/4$ pound shrimp or crabmeat, chopped

10 dried Chinese black mushrooms

1 ounce bean threads

1 medium onion, finely chopped

1 carrot, shredded

$1/4$ pound bean sprouts

$1/2$ teaspoon ground black pepper

1 to 2 teaspoons fish sauce*

1 teaspoon sugar

1 cup lukewarm water

12 rice papers, quartered

6 cups vegetable oil for deep-frying

48 lettuce leaves

1 bunch fresh mint

1 cucumber, thinly sliced

Spring Roll Sauce (recipe page 120)

In a medium bowl combine pork and shrimp. Soak mushrooms in warm water for 20 minutes; remove stems and chop caps. Soak bean threads in warm water for 20 minutes, then cut into 1-inch lengths. Add mushrooms, bean threads, onion, carrot, bean sprouts, black pepper and fish sauce to pork mixture; mix well. Set mixture aside for 15 minutes to allow flavors of ingredients to blend. Dilute sugar in lukewarm water. Place rice paper on a flat surface and brush with lukewarm water until it is pliable. Place 2 teaspoons of filling near the edge of the rice paper, then fold rice paper over the filling. Fold the right side over to enclose filling, then fold over left side. Continue to roll, then seal. Repeat for remaining wrappers. Heat oil for deep-frying to 375°F. Deep-fry a few rolls at a time until crisp and golden brown, about 10 minutes. Fry the remaining rolls. Serve by placing a spring roll in a lettuce leaf and top with mint and cucumber slices. Serve with Spring Roll Sauce. Accompany with chile sauce and chopped peanuts, if desired.

Technique for Wrapping Spring Rolls (refer to page 184)

*The amount of fish sauce used in the recipe depends on the brand selected and personal taste.

MAKES 48

Fish Patties

Fish Patties, sometimes called "fish cakes" in Thailand, are very popular appetizers usually accompanied with a chilled Thai beer. Fresh opakapaka or other firm white fish is finely minced and blended with string beans and Thai spices. Deep-fry and serve with Cucumber Sauce for dipping.

$1/2$ pound firm white fish fillet

3 ounces fresh string beans, finely chopped

1 onion, finely chopped

1 stalk fresh lemongrass, finely chopped

1 tablespoon finely chopped Chinese parsley

1 to 2 teaspoons seeded and finely chopped red chile peppers

1 to 2 tablespoons fish sauce*

1 egg

2 tablespoons cornstarch

$1/4$ teaspoon sugar

5 cups vegetable oil for deep-frying

Cucumber Sauce (recipe page 121)

Mince fish fillet in the bowl of a food processor. Combine fish, string beans, onion, lemongrass, Chinese parsley, red chile peppers, fish sauce, egg, cornstarch and sugar; blend well. Preheat oil for deep-frying to medium heat. Shape fish mixture into patties 2 inches in diameter and $1/2$ inch thick. Fry 10 to 15 minutes, or until golden brown. Drain on absorbent paper towels. Serve with Cucumber Sauce.

The amount of fish sauce used in the recipe depends on the brand selected and personal taste.

MAKES 4 TO 6 SERVINGS

Shrimp Rolls

Shrimp Rolls are very similar to Spring Rolls, except that they are wrapped in tofu sheets instead of rice papers. Steam first before deep-frying. Usually an hors d'oeuvre, they can be served as a main course.

12 large sheets dried tofu

1 pound shrimp

2 ounces crabmeat, chopped

1 ounce ground pork

1 to 2 ounces Chinese parsley sprigs, finely chopped

2 cloves garlic, finely chopped

$1/2$ teaspoon finely chopped common ginger

2 tablespoons cornstarch

1 to 2 tablespoons fish sauce*

$1/4$ teaspoon ground black pepper

5 cups vegetable oil for deep-frying

Spring Roll Sauce (recipe page 120) or Sriracha sauce

Soak tofu sheets in warm water for 15 minutes to soften, then drain and set aside individual sheets on a flat surface. Shell and devein shrimp; finely chopped. Combine shrimp, crab, pork, Chinese parsley, garlic, ginger, cornstarch, fish sauce and black pepper; blend well. Shape shrimp mixture into cylinders and place on tofu sheets near their edge. Fold tofu sheet over the filling by folding the right side over to enclose filling, then folding over the left side. Repeat for remaining wrappers. Steam for 15 minutes, then set aside to cool. Preheat oil for deep-frying to medium heat. Deep-fry for 10 to 12 minutes, or until golden brown. Drain on absorbent paper towels. Slice each roll crosswise and serve with Spring Roll Sauce or Sriracha sauce.

The amount of fish sauce used in the recipe depends on the brand selected and personal taste.

MAKES 4 TO 6 SERVINGS

Crisp Noodles

ILLUSTRATED ON OPPOSITE PAGE

The original Thai dish. Crisp and sweet small noodles that will melt in your mouth tossed with diced chicken and shrimp and flavorful tamarind sauce, an excellent introduction to Thai cuisine.

$1/4$ pound boneless chicken breast

2 ounces shrimp (optional)

$1/2$ cup dried tamarind

$1/2$ cup warm water

1 teaspoon catsup

1 to 3 tablespoons fish sauce*

1 tablespoon red wine vinegar

$1/3$ cup brown sugar

5 cups vegetable oil for deep-frying

$1/2$ cup bean sprouts

1 green onion, chopped

4 ounces rice noodles

Garnish: 4 to 5 sprigs Chinese parsley

Red chile flowers (directions page 179)

Dice chicken. Shell and devein shrimp; dice. Combine tamarind and warm water; blend well and strain. In a large saucepan combine chicken, shrimp, tamarind water, catsup, fish sauce, wine vinegar and brown sugar; bring to a boil over high heat. Immediately reduce heat to low and simmer for 1 hour. Set sauce aside to cool. In a wok, heat oil for deep-frying on high heat. Fry rice noodles; a little at a time, until they puff up. Place noodles on absorbent paper towels to drain. Combine noodles, sauce, bean sprouts, and green onions; toss lightly to mix. Garnish with Chinese parsley and red chile peppers. Serve immediately, since noodles soften with 10 minutes after combining with sauce.

*The amount of fish sauce used in the recipe depends on the brand selected and personal taste.

MAKES 6 TO 8 SERVINGS

Stuffed Tofu

Tofu, also called bean curd or bean cake, is made from soybeans and is available in many forms. This recipe uses deep-fried tofu cubes that are stuffed with a flavorful pork mixture.

6 ounces ground lean pork

2 cloves garlic, finely chopped

$1/4$ cup chopped green onions

2 tablespoons chopped Chinese parsley

$1/4$ teaspoon salt

$1/8$ teaspoon freshly ground black pepper

1 teaspoon cornstarch

8 pieces (approximately 2 ounces each) deep-fried tofu

2 cups vegetable oil for deep-frying

Spring Roll Sauce (recipe page 120)

Garnish: Red chile pepper

Chinese parsley sprigs

In a large bowl combine pork, garlic, green onions, Chinese parsley, salt, black pepper and cornstarch; blend well. Make a hole in each tofu cube with the tip of a knife and stuff the pork mixture into the opening. Heat oil on medium and deep fry stuffed tofu until golden brown. Drain on absorbent paper towels. Serve with Spring Roll Sauce. Garnish with red chile pepper and Chinese parsley sprigs. Serve hot.

MAKES 4 SERVINGS

Bangkok Stuffed Wings

These deboned chicken wings are filled with a beautiful blend of chicken, mushrooms, carrots, long rice, onion, water chestnuts and spices. They can be steamed and frozen, ready to deep fry golden brown just before serving.

4 pounds chicken wings

1 pound shrimp

1 ounce bean threads

2 carrots, shredded

$1/4$ cup water chestnuts

1 onion

2 to 4 tablespoons fish sauce*

2 to 3 cloves garlic

$1/4$ teaspoon ground black pepper

1 tablespoon Chinese parsley roots

1 cup rice flour or cornstarch

5 cups vegetable oil for deep-frying

Satay Sauce (recipe page 119) or Sriracha sauce

Debone chicken wings according to method shown on page 185. Shell and devein shrimp. Soak bean threads in warm water for 15 minutes; drain and cut into 1-inch lengths. In a food processor combine chicken meat obtaining from deboning, shrimp, carrots, water chestnuts, onion, fish sauce, garlic, black pepper and Chinese parsley roots; blend until smooth. Stir in bean threads. Stuff chicken mixture loosely into the wings. Steam about 20 minutes, or until almost cooked. They can be frozen at this point and deep-fried when ready to serve. Coat wings with rice flour. Heat oil for deep-frying to 375°F. Deep-fry wings until golden brown. Serve warm with Satay Sauce or Sriracha sauce.

Technique for Deboning Chicken Wings (refer to page 185)

*The amount of fish sauce used in the recipe depends on the brand selected and personal taste.

MAKES 6 TO 8 SERVINGS

Summer Rolls

ILLUSTRATED ON OPPOSITE PAGE

In Thailand, these are referred to as "Fresh Spring Rolls" and are very popular among the Bangkok Thai. This is the Thai version of a Vietnamese dish. Fresh steamed shrimp, chicken, and fresh vegetables are wrapped in soft rice paper and served with either Spring Roll Sauce or hoisin sauce.

10 rice papers (10 to 12 inches in diameter)

3 cups lukewarm water

10 large shrimp, steamed and shelled

1 boneless chicken breast, steamed and sliced in 1-inch strips

1 cucumber, shredded

1 carrot or daikon, shredded

10 to 15 Chinese parsley sprigs

10 to 15 mint leaves

$1/2$ cup cooked rice noodles (optional)

Spring Roll Sauce (recipe page 120) or hoisin sauce

1 tablespoon coarsely chopped peanuts

Garnish: Pickled shredded carrot and daikon

2 to 3 fresh red chile peppers, sliced

Mint leaves

Place rice paper on a flat surface and lightly brush with lukewarm water until it becomes pliable. Cut shrimp in half lengthwise. Place two shrimp halves and a portion of the chicken, cucumber, carrot, Chinese parsley, mint, and rice noodles near one edge of the rice paper. Fold the rice paper over the filling. Fold the right side over to enclose filling. Then fold over left side. Continue to roll. Then seal. Repeat for remaining wrappers. Serve whole or cut the rolls in half at an angle. Serve with Spring Roll Sauce or hoisin sauce. Sprinkle sauce with peanuts before serving. Garnish with carrot and daikon, chile peppers and mint leaves.

MAKES 10 ROLLS

Crisp Fried Crab Claws

These crab claws with a crispy coating of rice flour, lemongrass, and red chiles make a delicious appetizer.

8 large crab claws

$1/4$ cup rice flour

2 tablespoons cornstarch

$1/2$ teaspoon sugar or honey

1 stalk fresh lemongrass, finely chopped

4 cloves garlic, finely chopped

1 tablespoon finely chopped
    Chinese parsley

1 to 2 teaspoons seeded and finely
    chopped red chile peppers
    (optional)

1 teaspoon soy sauce

1 egg

1 to 2 teaspoons fish sauce*

$1/4$ teaspoon freshly ground
    black pepper

$1/4$ cup cold water

5 cups vegetable oil for deep-frying

Spring Roll Sauce (recipe page 120)

Garnish: Lettuce leaves (optional)

Rinse crab claws and pat dry. Combine rice flour, cornstarch, sugar, lemongrass, garlic, Chinese parsley, red chile peppers, soy sauce, egg, fish sauce, and black pepper; blend well. Stir in cold water and mix well. Preheat oil for deep-frying on medium heat. Coat crab claws with rice flour mixture. Deep-fry for 12 to 15 minutes, or until golden brown. Drain on absorbent paper towels. Serve with Spring Roll Sauce. Garnish with lettuce leaves.

*The amount of fish sauce used in the recipe depends on the brand selected and personal taste.

MAKES 4 SERVINGS

Crispy Fried Shrimp

This recipe is one of the most frequently asked for when guests dine in our restaurant. It's very easy to make and it's delicious. Like all deep-fried items, serve hot, immediately after it is cooked.

1 pound large shrimp

1 cup tapioca flour or cornstarch

2 ounces Thai long-grain rice noodles, cut into 2- to 3-inch strips

$^1/_4$ teaspoon salt

4 cups vegetable oil for deep-frying

6 tablespoons Spring Roll Sauce (recipe page 120) or Sriracha sauce

Garnish: Lettuce leaves

Cucumber slices

Red chile peppers, sliced

Chinese parsley sprigs

Shell and devein shrimp, leaving the tails on for color. In a mixing bowl, combine tapioca flour, rice noodles, and salt; mix lightly. Roll each shrimp in the flour mixture to coat and set aside. Just before serving, heat oil in a wok on high heat. Place the shrimp 1 at a time in the oil and fry for about 2 minutes, or until the shrimp are cooked. Remove shrimp and place on absorbent paper towels. Serve hot with Spring Roll Sauce. Garnish with lettuce, cucumber slices, red chile peppers, and Chinese parsley sprigs.

MAKES 4 TO 6 SERVINGS

Satay on Skewers

ILLUSTRATED ON OPPOSITE PAGE

Satay originally was an Indonesian specialty. You will find the Thai version a little bit spicier than the Indonesian.

    1 pound boneless chicken, beef or pork, or a combination

    3 tablespoons vegetable oil

    1 stalk fresh lemongrass

    3 cloves garlic

    $1/2$ teaspoon seeded and finely chopped red chile peppers

    1 tablespoon curry powder

    1 teaspoon sugar or honey

    $1/2$ to 1 teaspoon fish sauce*

    Skewers

    Satay Sauce (recipe page 119)

    Cucumber Sauce (recipe page 121)

Cut chicken thinly into 2-inch strips. In a food processor or blender combine oil, lemongrass, garlic, red chile peppers, curry powder, sugar and fish sauce; blend until smooth. Pour over chicken; marinate for 2 hours. Thread chicken onto skewers and barbecue or broil, turning occasionally, until cooked. Serve with Satay Sauce and Cucumber Sauce.

The amount of fish sauce used in the recipe depends on the brand selected and personal taste.

MAKES 4 SERVINGS

Son-in-Law Eggs

Son-in-Law Eggs is a direct translation of the Thai name for this dish. These are hard-boiled eggs deep fried and covered with a sweet palm sugar sauce.

6 hard-boiled eggs

2 cups vegetable oil

4 shallots, finely chopped

2 cloves garlic, finely chopped

2 tablespoons palm sugar or brown sugar

$^1/_4$ cup hot water

1 to 2 teaspoons fish sauce*

4 lettuce leaves

Garnish: Chinese parsley sprigs

Green onions, cut into 2-inch lengths

Peel hard-boiled eggs. Heat oil in a wok on medium heat and deep-fry eggs until golden brown. Set eggs aside to cool for 20 minutes, then cut eggs into quarters. In 1 tablespoon of the oil stir-fry shallots and garlic until golden brown; drain on absorbent paper towels. In a saucepan dissolve palm sugar in hot water; add fish sauce and mix well for 3 minutes. Stir in shallots and garlic. To serve, arrange lettuce leaves on a large platter and top with egg quarters and pour sauce over the top. Garnish with Chinese parsley and green onions.

*The amount of fish sauce used in the recipe depends on the brand selected and personal taste.

MAKES 6 SERVINGS

Salted Eggs

There are villages in Thailand where refrigeration is not available, so farmers preserve their meat, poultry, seafood, vegetables and eggs by methods of pickling, salting, drying or fermenting. Today, these delicacies are very much in demand in gourmet stores and markets in Thailand cities.

2 cups salt
4 cups hot water
12 eggs

In a 1-gallon glass jar, dissolve salt in hot water; set aside to cool. Place eggs into the salt water; cover with a tight-fitting lid and let soak for 6 weeks. After 6 weeks, drain off salt water. Hard-boil all the eggs and refrigerate. Keep shells on until ready to serve.

Crisp Fried Tofu

ILLUSTRATED ON OPPOSITE PAGE

"French-fried" fresh tofu served with a spicy Spring Roll Sauce, Satay Sauce, crisp lettuce and cool, refreshing cucumber slices—a delightful appetizer.

$1/2$ pound tofu

$1/4$ cup rice flour

2 tablespoons cornstarch

5 cups vegetable oil for deep-frying

Spring Roll Sauce (recipe page 120)

Satay Sauce (recipe page 119)

Lettuce leaves

Cucumber slices

Garnish: Chinese parsley sprigs

Cut tofu into strips 2 x 1 x $1/4$ inches. Combine rice flour and cornstarch. Preheat oil for deep-frying on medium heat. Coat tofu with rice flour mixture. Deep-fry for 7 to 10 minutes, or until golden brown. Drain on absorbent paper towels. Serve with Spring Roll Sauce, Satay Sauce, lettuce leaves and cucumber slices. Garnish with Chinese parsley.

MAKES 3 TO 4 SERVINGS

Soups

Spicy Shrimp Soup with Lemongrass

ILLUSTRATED ON OPPOSITE PAGE

A classic Thai seafood soup. Quick and easy to prepare, it's the most popular soup in Thailand. The lemongrass and kaffir lime leaves are for flavor only, and shouldn't be eaten.

$1/2$ pound shrimp

4 cups water

1 stalk fresh lemongrass, sliced

1 can (8 oz.) straw mushrooms, drained

2 kaffir lime leaves

1 to 3 tablespoons fish sauce*

$1/4$ cup fresh lime juice

2 tablespoons sliced green onions

1 tablespoon chopped Chinese parsley

1 to 4 red chile peppers, seeded and chopped, or $1/2$ teaspoon red chile paste

Garnish: Chinese parsley sprigs

Devein shrimp; leave tails on for color, if desired. Bring water to a boil. Add lemongrass and straw mushrooms; immediately reduce heat to medium-low. Add shrimp and cook for 3 minutes; stir in fish sauce and lime juice. Sprinkle with green onions, Chinese parsley, red chile peppers, if desired. Serve hot. Garnish with Chinese parsley sprigs.

Note: Fresh mushrooms can be substituted for the canned mushrooms, but add at end of cooking time.

Idea: Spicy Thai Vegetable Soup can be prepared by substituting tofu and mixed vegetables for the shrimp. Use $1/2$ teaspoon of salt instead of the fish sauce.

*The amount of fish sauce used in the recipe depends on the brand selected and personal taste.

MAKES 4 SERVINGS

Thai Ginger Chicken Soup

Thai ginger with tender slices of light chicken meat simmer in coconut milk with green onions and spices. Mild.

$1/2$ pound boneless chicken breasts

3 cups coconut milk

2 cups water

1-inch section kha (Thai ginger), thinly sliced

1 to 3 tablespoons fish sauce*

$1/4$ cup fresh lime juice

2 tablespoons sliced green onions

1 tablespoon chopped Chinese parsley

Garnish: 1 to 3 red chile peppers, seeded and slivered

Chinese parsley sprigs

Cut chicken into thin strips. Bring coconut milk and water to a boil. Reduce heat to medium-low; add chicken and cook for 3 minutes. Stir in Thai ginger, fish sauce and lime juice. Sprinkle with green onions and Chinese parsley. Serve hot. Garnish with red chile peppers and Chinese parsley sprigs.

Note: Fresh common ginger can be substituted for kha.

*The amount of fish sauce used in the recipe depends on the brand selected and personal taste.

MAKES 4 SERVINGS

Thai Soup Stock

Rice and noodle soups are often considered as a full meal in Thailand and are derived from Chinese. In fact, the Thai words for noodles, "Gway-tio, mee," are Chinese. Soups vary greatly depending on the main ingredients and soup stock. Cooked rice or noodles are added along with various garnishings.

6 cups water

1 pound chicken bones or beef bones, or white radish for a vegetarian stock

1-inch section common ginger, thinly sliced

4 to 5 Chinese parsley roots

1 whole onion, quartered

1 teaspoon salt

In a stockpot bring water to a boil. Add chicken bones, ginger, Chinese parsley roots, onion and salt. Reduce heat and simmer for $1/2$ hour. Strain stock and reserve for use in the following soups.

Rice Soup

ILLUSTRATED ON PAGES 40 AND 41

Rice soup in Thailand is usually spicier and thinner than the Chinese version.

5 cups Thai Soup Stock (recipe page 39)

$1/4$ cup minced beef, chicken, pork, fish or shrimp

1 tablespoon minced common ginger

$2^1/2$ cups cooked rice

1 to 2 tablespoons fish sauce*

1 egg

Garnish: 2 green onions, thinly sliced

1 tablespoon chopped Chinese parsley

1 tablespoon fried onion or garlic flakes

1 teaspoon dried red chile pepper flakes (optional)

In a stockpot heat Thai Soup Stock. Add minced meat or seafood and ginger; bring to a boil, stirring occasionally. Reduce heat to simmer. Add rice and cook for 2 minutes. Season with fish sauce. Break egg into a serving bowl and beat lightly. Pour soup on top of the egg. Garnish with green onions, Chinese parsley, onion flakes and red chile flakes. Serve hot.

*The amount of fish sauce used in the recipe depends on the brand selected and personal taste.

MAKES 6 SERVINGS

Thai Chicken Soup with Bean Threads

ILLUSTRATED ON PAGE 41

This very mild chicken soup with bean thread is popular among the Chinese Thai.

$1/4$ pound bean threads

$1/2$ pound boneless chicken breasts, thinly sliced

5 cups Thai Soup Stock (recipe page 39)

4 oz. straw mushrooms, drained

4 oz. young corn, drained

2 oz. water chestnuts, thinly sliced

$1/4$ cup shredded bamboo shoots

2 stalks green onions, cut into 2-inch lengths

Garnish: Chinese parsley sprigs

Soak bean threads in warm water for 15 minutes; drain. Shred chicken. Bring soup stock to a boil. Add chicken, bean threads, straw mushrooms, young corn, water chestnuts, bamboo shoots and green onions. Reduce heat and simmer 3 to 5 minutes. Garnish with Chinese parsley.

MAKES 6 SERVINGS

Thai Noodle Soup with Beef Meatballs

ILLUSTRATED ON OPPOSITE PAGE

This Thai noodle soup with meatballs is a popular snack, particularly among the students.

1/4 pound rice noodles

5 cups Thai Soup Stock (recipe page 39)

1/2 pound beef meatballs
    or shredded beef

2 ounces bean sprouts

1 to 2 teaspoons fish sauce

Garnish: Chinese parsley sprigs

2 tablespoons thinly sliced green onions

1 teaspoons chopped fresh red chile
    peppers or ground red chile peppers

Soak rice noodles in warm water for 15 minutes; drain. Bring stock to a boil. Add rice noodles, meatballs, bean sprouts and fish sauce. Reduce heat and simmer for 5 to 7 minutes. Garnish with Chinese parsley sprigs, green onions and red chile peppers.

A.   Thai Noodle Soup with Beef Meatballs
B.   Egg Noodle Soup with Char Siu
C.   Thai Noodle Soup with Chicken
D.   Egg Noodles
E.   Rice Noodles

Clockwise from top left: Thai Noodle Soup with Beef Meatballs, Thai Noodle Soup with Chicken (page 47), and Egg Noodle Soup with Char Siu (page 46)

MAKES 6 SERVINGS

Egg Noodle Soup with Char Siu

ILLUSTRATED ON PAGE 44

Egg noodle soup with clear broth is more popular among city folks than the villagers.

$^1/_2$ pound char siu (Chinese barbecued pork)

5 cups Thai Soup Stock (recipe page 39)

$^1/_4$ pound egg noodles

2 ounces bean sprouts

1 to 2 teaspoons fish sauce*

Garnish: Chinese parsley sprigs

2 tablespoons thinly sliced green onions

1 teaspoon dried red chile pepper flakes (optional)

Thinly slice char siu. Bring stock to a boil. Add noodles, char siu, bean sprouts and fish sauce. Reduce heat and simmer for 3 to 5 minutes. Garnish with Chinese parsley sprigs, green onions and red chile pepper flakes.

*The amount of fish sauce used in the recipe depends on the brand selected and personal taste.

MAKES 3 TO 4 SERVINGS

Thai Noodle Soup with Chicken

ILLUSTRATED ON PAGE 44

Boneless chicken and fresh bean sprouts make this a nice variation of Thai noodle soup.

$^1/_4$ pound rice noodles

5 cups Thai Soup Stock (recipe page 39)

$^1/_2$ pound boneless chicken breasts

2 ounces bean sprouts

1 to 2 teaspoons fish sauce*

Garnish: Chinese parsley sprigs

2 tablespoons chopped green onions

1 teaspoon seeded and chopped red chile peppers
    or ground red chile peppers (optional)

Soak rice noodles in warm water for 15 minutes; drain. Bring stock to a boil. Add rice noodles, chicken, bean sprouts and fish sauce. Reduce heat and simmer for 5 to 7 minutes. Garnish with Chinese parsley sprigs, green onions and red chile peppers.

The amount of fish sauce used in the recipe depends on the brand selected and personal taste.

Makes 3 to 6 servings

Salads

Chieng Mai Chicken Salad *51*

Cucumber Salad *52*

Thai Beef Salad *53*

Calamari Salad with Fresh Lemongrass *55*

Green Papaya Salad *56*

Roast Duck Salad *57*

Chieng Mai Chicken Salad

ILLUSTRATED ON OPPOSITE PAGE

Chieng Mai is a northeastern city in Thailand, culturally very close to Laos, and famous for its chicken salad, which was originally called "laap." Laotians make their laap with beef, chicken or pork, using the liver, gizzard, tripe and skin. Uncooked freshwater fish and shrimp with anchovy and lime juice are other variations.

1 pound boneless chicken, ground

1 stalk fresh lemongrass, finely chopped

3 kaffir lime leaves, finely chopped

3 to 6 red chile peppers, seeded and chopped (optional)

$1/4$ cup fresh lime juice

1 to 2 tablespoons fish sauce*

1 tablespoon ground roasted rice**

1 green onion, thinly sliced

6 to 8 sprigs Chinese parsley, chopped

12 mint leaves, chopped

1 teaspoon ground red chile peppers (optional)

Lettuce leaves or cabbage squares

Garnish: Green onions, thinly sliced
Mint leaves

Heat a small skillet and cook chicken in a little water, but without oil, stirring constantly. Set chicken aside to cool. In a bowl combine chicken, lemongrass, kaffir lime leaves, chopped red chile peppers, lime juice and fish sauce; mix well. Stir in ground roasted rice, green onion, chopped Chinese parsley and chopped mint leaves. Transfer to a platter and serve at room temperature with lettuce leaves. Garnish with green onions and mint leaves.

*The amount of fish sauce used in the recipe depends on the brand selected and personal taste.

**To prepare ground roasted rice, place rice in heavy pan over medium heat. Carefully brown the rice until very dark brown. Set aside to cool. Place in blender or spice mill and reduce to a fine powder. Store in an airtight container.

MAKES 6 SERVINGS

Cucumber Salad

This cucumber salad is one of the favorite noontime snacks for farmers.

    2 large cucumbers

    2 red chile peppers, seeded and chopped

    1 clove garlic, minced

    $1/2$ to 1 tablespoon fish sauce* or anchovy paste

    2 to 3 tablespoons fresh lime juice

    $1/2$ teaspoon ground dried shrimp

Shred cucumbers. In a large bowl combine shredded cucumber and all the remaining ingredients; toss lightly to mix. Serve immediately to prevent ingredients from marinating.

Note: Long string beans cut into 2-inch strips can be substituted for the shredded cucumbers.

*The amount of fish sauce used in the recipe depends on the brand selected and personal taste.

MAKES 4 SERVINGS

Thai Beef Salad

ILLUSTRATED ON PAGE 54

A spicy dressing tossed with thinly sliced strips of cooked roast beef and other classic Thai ingredients…results are superb and very popular.

1 pound cooked roast beef

$^1/_4$ ounce bean threads

1 onion, thinly sliced

1 small cucumber, thinly sliced

1 stalk fresh lemongrass, thinly sliced

$^1/_4$ cup fresh lime juice

1 to 2 tablespoons fish sauce*

2 to 4 red chile peppers, seeded and chopped (optional)

10 to 15 mint leaves

2 green onions, thinly sliced

Garnish: Green onion brushes (directions page 183)

Lime

Radish roses (optional)

Mint leaves

Thinly slice roast beef into 2-inch strips. Soak bean threads in warm water for 15 minutes; drain and cut into 3-inch lengths. In a large bowl combine roast beef, bean threads, onion, cucumber, lemongrass, lime juice, fish sauce, red chile peppers, mint leaves and chopped green onions; toss to mix well. Garnish with green onion brushes, lime, radish roses and mint leaves. Serve chilled or near room temperature.

*The amount of fish sauce used in the recipe depends on the brand selected and personal taste.

MAKES 6 SERVINGS

Calamari Salad with Fresh Lemongrass

ILLUSTRATED ON OPPOSITE PAGE

Calamari dishes are very popular in Southern Thailand and Bangkok. Calamari is available fresh, frozen, dried and pickled. Fresh calamari is best for salads, but frozen is acceptable. All Thai salads are served chilled or near room temperature and are prepared just before serving to prevent dressing from marinating the main ingredients.

1 pound calamari (squid)

1/4 ounce bean threads

1/3 cup water

1 stalk fresh lemongrass, finely chopped

3 fresh kaffir lime leaves, finely chopped

1 onion, thinly sliced

5 teaspoons fresh lime juice

1/2 to 1 tablespoon fish sauce*

1 to 5 red chile peppers, seeded and chopped (optional)

15 to 20 mint leaves

6 to 8 sprigs Chinese parsley, chopped

1 green onion, thinly sliced

3 to 5 lettuce leaves (optional)

Garnish: Red chile flowers (directions page 179)

Lime

Rinse calamari well in cold water. Soak bean threads in warm water for 15 minutes; drain and cut into 3-inch lengths. Prepare calamari according to technique on page 186. In a small saucepan bring water to a boil and add calamari. Cook for 3 to 5 minutes or until opaque; drain. Set aside for a few minutes to cool. Combine lemongrass, kaffir lime leaves, onion, lime juice, fish sauce and red chile peppers. Just before serving combine calamari, dressing, bean threads, mint, chopped Chinese parsley and green onion; toss to mix well. Serve with lettuce leaves, if desired. Garnish with red chile pepper flowers and lime. Serve chilled or near room temperature.

Technique for Cleaning and Scoring Squid (refer to page 186)

*The amount of fish sauce used in the recipe depends on the brand selected and personal taste.

MAKES 6 SERVINGS

Top: Calamari Salad with
Fresh Lemongrass (page 55)
Bottom: Thai Beef Salad (page 53)

Green Papaya Salad

A packet-type salad—easy to make, fun to eat.

$1/2$ pound green papaya

1 clove garlic

2 to 3 red chile peppers, seeded

1 tomato, sliced

1 to 2 tablespoons fish sauce*

3 tablespoons lime juice

Lettuce leaves or cabbage squares

1 lime, cut into wedges

Garnish: Red chile peppers (optional)

Peel and seed papaya; shred. Grind together garlic and red chile peppers in a food processor or mortar. Mix together the papaya, tomato, fish sauce and lime juice; add in garlic mixture and toss lightly. Place a portion of papaya mixture onto a lettuce leaf or cabbage square and form into a packet to eat. Serve with wedges of lime. Garnish with red chile peppers.

Note: Shredded carrots or cucumber can be substituted for the green papaya.

Idea: There are many variations of papaya salad in Southeast Asia. Thais like theirs with ground peanuts, sugar and salted shrimp powder. The Laotian version usually called for pickled freshwater crabs and long string beans. Vietnamese like theirs with beef jerky and mint leaves.

*The amount of fish sauce used in the recipe depends on the brand selected and personal taste.

MAKES 4 SERVINGS

Roast Duck Salad

In Thailand, roast duck is quite popular among city folks, and you can find it everywhere, from coffee shops to food courts, in any city. Thinly sliced strips of boneless roast duck with roasted chile paste and lime juice make wonderful use of this favorite Thai ingredient.

1 tablespoon Thai roasted chile paste

2 teaspoons fish sauce

6 tablespoons lime juice

2 cups thinly sliced boneless roast duck

1 cucumber, sliced

$^1/_3$ round onion, thinly sliced

$^1/_4$ cup chopped celery

$^1/_4$ cup chopped Chinese parsley

20 mint leaves

Garnish: Cashew nuts (optional)

1 fresh red chile pepper, chopped (optional)

Chinese parsley sprigs

Mint leaves

Combine roasted chile paste, fish sauce, and lime juice in a mixing bowl; blend well. Just before serving toss together roast duck, cucumber, onion, celery, Chinese parsley, mint leaves, and chile pepper. Add dressing just before serving to prevent dressing from marinating the ingredients; toss lightly. Serve at room temperature. Garnish with cashew nuts, red chile peppers, Chinese parsley sprigs, and mint leaves.

MAKES 4 SERVINGS

Seafood, Poultry and Meat

Steamed Clams with Fresh Ginger **60**

Stuffed Crab **61**

Steamed Fish in Banana Leaves **62**

Asparagus with Shrimp and Black Mushrooms **63**

Thai Shrimp with Garlic **64**

Shrimp with Red Chile Paste **65**

Satay Shrimp **67**

Steamed Fish Eggs with Dill **68**

Thai Sweet-and-Sour Fish **69**

Whole Fish with Fresh Ginger and Yellow Bean Sauce **72**

Opakapaka with Red Curry Sauce **73**

Crab Legs with Yellow Bean Sauce **76**

Lobster with Pineapple **77**

Scallops with Fresh Basil **80**

Shrimp with Mixed Vegetables **81**

Fried Mussels with Fresh Whole Chile Peppers **84**

Pork Chops with Lemongrass and Garlic **87**

Honey Glazed Spareribs **85**

Chicken with Fresh Sweet Basil **88**

Bar-B-Que Chicken **89**

Evil Jungle Prince with Chicken **92**

Thai Roast Duck **93**

Eggplant with Chicken **95**

Roast Duck with Chile **96**

Chicken with Black Mushrooms **97**

Cashew Chicken **99**

Beef with String Beans and Fresh Ginger **100**

Beef with Fresh Sweet Basil **101**

Beef with Oyster Sauce **104**

Crispy Fried Beef **105**

Steamed Clams with Fresh Ginger

ILLUSTRATED ON PAGE 83

Seafood is abundant in Thailand, especially at all the beach resorts. This combination of clams with fresh ginger is delicious and simple.

> 2 pounds fresh clams
>
> 2 cloves garlic, chopped
>
> $1/2$ onion, thinly sliced
>
> 3 green onions, cut into 2-inch lengths
>
> 2 tablespoons thinly slivered ginger
>
> 1 to 2 tablespoons yellow bean sauce*
>
> 1 tablespoon oyster sauce
>
> 1 to 2 red chile peppers, seeded and cut into thin strips (optional)

Rinse clams. Combine all the remaining ingredients to make a sauce. Pour sauce over clams and mix well. Steam for 15 minutes, or until clams open up. Serve hot.

Yellow bean sauce from Thailand is saltier than sauce from Hong Kong or China. Season to taste.

MAKES 4 SERVINGS

Stuffed Crab

A sensational seafood dish, everybody's favorite, stuffed crab shells with fresh crabmeat, shrimp, mushrooms, long rice and other vegetables make a delicious meal.

5 large crabs

4 ounces dried Chinese black mushrooms

2 ounces bean threads

6 ounces shrimp, shelled and deveined

1 onion, chopped

1 carrot, shredded

6 water chestnuts, chopped

1 egg

$1/2$ teaspoon cornstarch

2 teaspoons fish sauce

$1/4$ teaspoon ground black pepper

6 cups vegetable oil for deep-frying

Garnish: Spring Roll Sauce (recipe page 120)

Green onions

Red chile flowers (directions page 179)

Steam whole crabs for about 30 minutes, or until cooked. Remove crabmeat from shells and set shells aside. Soak Chinese black mushrooms and bean threads in warm water in separate containers for 15 minutes. Drain Chinese black mushrooms; discard stems and finely chop. Drain bean threads and cut into 1-inch lengths. Finely chop crabmeat and shrimp. Combine crabmeat, shrimp, Chinese black mushrooms, bean threads, onion, carrot, water chestnuts, egg, cornstarch, fish sauce and pepper; blend well. Stuff shells with crabmeat mixture. Heat oil for deep-frying to medium heat. Deep-fry shells for 12 to 15 minutes, or until golden brown. Drain on absorbent paper towels. Serve with Spring Roll Sauce. Garnish with green onions and red chile flowers.

MAKES 4 SERVINGS

Steamed Fish in Banana Leaves

In this healthy, light dish, pieces of fresh fish or chicken and spices are wrapped in banana leaves, then steamed.

2 pounds firm white fish fillet

2 pounds apple banana leaves

1 tablespoon Red Curry Paste (recipe page 126)

$^1/_3$ cup coconut milk

2 eggs

3 tablespoons finely chopped lemongrass

$^1/_4$ cup fish sauce

5 fresh red chile peppers, seeded and chopped (optional)

15 lemon basil leaves (optional)

1 ounce fresh dill, chopped

6 kaffir lime leaves, finely chopped

$^1/_4$ cup chopped shallots

3 tablespoons chopped Chinese parsley roots

2 tablespoons rice flour

Garnish: Coconut milk

Red chile peppers

Chinese parsley sprigs

Cut fish fillet into bite-size pieces. Cut banana leaves into pieces and form into cups and fasten with toothpicks or use small rice bowls. In a mixing bowl combine red curry paste, coconut milk, and eggs; blend well. Stir in lemongrass, fish sauce, chile peppers, lemon basil leaves, dill, kaffir lime leaves, shallots, Chinese parsley roots, and rice flour. Pour mixture over fish and blend well. Spoon fish mixture into banana leaf cups or small rice bowls. Steam for 45 minutes on medium heat, or until cooked, depending on the depth of the cup or bowl. Garnish each serving with coconut milk, red chile peppers, and Chinese parsley sprigs.

MAKES 4 TO 6 SERVINGS

Asparagus with Shrimp and Black Mushrooms

Asparagus is very popular among the Chinese Thai in Bangkok. This combination of asparagus with Chinese black mushrooms is a delicious and a simple dish to prepare. For hot-food lovers, add a few chile peppers.

$^1/_2$ pound shrimp

1 pound fresh asparagus

1 ounce dried Chinese black mushrooms

2 tablespoons vegetable oil

2 cloves garlic, minced

3 tablespoons oyster sauce

2 to 4 red chile peppers, seeded and sliced (optional)

Method 1: Shell and devein shrimp; set aside. Rinse asparagus; peel and trim stems. Cut into 3-inch lengths. Soak mushrooms in warm water for 15 minutes; drain and discard stems. Slice caps into 1-inch strips. In a skillet heat oil; add garlic and cook until light brown. Stir in mushrooms and cook, stirring constantly, for 1 minute. Add shrimp, asparagus, oyster sauce and red chile peppers; stir-fry for 3 minutes. Serve hot.

Method 2: Shell and devein shrimp; set aside. Rinse asparagus; peel and trim stems. Soak mushrooms in warm water for 15 minutes; drain and discard stems. Leave caps whole. Steam shrimp, asparagus and mushrooms for 10 minutes, or until the shrimp are cooked. Remove from steamer and arrange on a platter. In a skillet heat oil; add garlic and cook until light brown. Stir in oyster sauce, then pour over shrimp platter. Serve hot.

MAKES 3 TO 4 SERVINGS

Thai Shrimp with Garlic

Garlic and black pepper give this stir-fried dish the spicy goodness that Thais love so well. Asian garlic is slightly smaller and stronger in fragrance than the Western variety.

$1/4$ cup vegetable oil

4 cloves garlic, finely chopped

$1/2$ pound shrimp, shelled and deveined

$1/4$ cup coconut milk

$1/4$ cup straw or fresh mushrooms

$1/4$ teaspoon ground black pepper

1 to 2 teaspoons fish sauce*

3 cups chopped cabbage

Garnish: Chinese parsley sprigs

Heat oil in a wok. Add garlic and stir-fry until garlic is golden brown. Stir in shrimp, coconut milk, mushrooms, black pepper and fish sauce; cook for about 10 minutes, or until shrimp are cooked. Line a platter with chopped cabbage and top with shrimp. Garnish with Chinese parsley.

The amount of fish sauce used in the recipe depends on the brand selected and personal taste.

MAKES 2 TO 3 SERVINGS

Shrimp with Red Chile Paste

Stir-fried shrimp with chile paste and fresh sweet basil leaves are a real classic of Thai home cooking.

1 pound medium shrimp

3 tablespoons vegetable oil

1 teaspoon red chile paste

1 to 3 tablespoons fish sauce*

1 teaspoon brown sugar or honey

20 sweet basil leaves

Shell and devein shrimp, leaving tails on for color. Heat oil in a wok on high heat with chile paste until it starts to bubble. Add shrimp, fish sauce and brown sugar; stir-fry for 3 to 5 minutes, or until shrimp are cooked. Stir in sweet basil leaves just before serving.

The amount of fish sauce used in the recipe depends on the brand selected and personal taste.

MAKES 3 TO 4 SERVINGS

Satay Shrimp

ILLUSTRATED ON OPPOSITE PAGE

An enticing shrimp dish in a superbly seasoned Thai peanut sauce.

1 pound shrimp

1/4 cup vegetable oil

2 cloves garlic, minced

1 onion, chopped

1/2 to 1 teaspoon ground dried
    red chile peppers

3 kaffir lime leaves

1/2 teaspoon curry powder

1 tablespoon chopped fresh lemongrass

1 cup coconut milk

1/2 cup milk

1 2-inch cinnamon stick

3 bay leaves

2 teaspoons tamarind sauce

1 to 3 tablespoons fish sauce*

3 tablespoons dark brown sugar

3 tablespoons lemon juice

1 cup chunky peanut butter

3 cups water

Garnish: 1 cup chopped cabbage

1 tomato, cut into wedges

Shell and devein shrimp; set aside. Heat oil in a skillet to medium-high heat and sauté garlic, onion, red chile peppers, kaffir lime leaves, curry powder and lemongrass for 2 to 3 minutes. Stir in coconut milk, milk, cinnamon stick, bay leaves, tamarind sauce, fish sauce, brown sugar, lemon juice and peanut butter; mix well. Reduce heat and cook, stirring frequently, until sauce thickens, about 30 minutes. Be very careful sauce does not stick to bottom of pan. Bring water to a boil; add shrimp and cook 3 minutes. Place chopped cabbage on serving platter and top with shrimp and tomato wedges. Pour on sauce.

The amount of fish sauce used in the recipe depends on the brand selected and personal taste.

MAKES 4 SERVINGS

Steamed Fish Eggs with Dill

Young dill leaves are often used in fish dishes in Northern Thailand and Laos. Thais call it "pak chee lao," meaning Laotian parsley. Eryngium foetidum is another edible leaf in Laotian cooking, and is also commonly used in Vietnam as a garnish for noodle soups. Caution…both dill and eryngium foetidum have very strong flavors.

2 cups fish eggs

2 ounces firm white fish fillet

$\frac{1}{8}$ teaspoon salt

3 dried red chile peppers

6 shallots, chopped

4 cloves garlic, finely chopped

1 ounce fresh dill, cut into 2-inch strips

5 eryngium foetidum leaves, finely chopped

2 to 4 tablespoons fish sauce*

1 teaspoon cornstarch

2 eggs

Garnish: Fresh dill

Rinse fish eggs in cold water, then set aside. Mince fish fillet; add salt and mix well. Remove seeds from dried red chile peppers, then soak in warm water for 5 minutes; drain and finely chop. Combine fish eggs, fish, red chile peppers, shallots, garlic, dill, eryngium foetidum leaves, fish sauce, cornstarch and eggs; blend well. Pour mixture into a 2-inch-deep pan and steam for 40 minutes. Serve warm. Garnish with fresh dill.

Note: Chopped shrimp can be substituted for the fish eggs. A gourmet delight, yet amazingly easy.

*The amount of fish sauce used in the recipe depends on the brand selected and personal taste.

MAKES 3 TO 4 SERVINGS

Thai Sweet-and-Sour Fish

Traditionally, this sweet-and-sour sauce has more vegetables and less cornstarch than the Chinese variety.

2 pounds whole snapper

4 tablespoons cornstarch

1 pound mixed vegetables (refer to page 81)

4 cups vegetable oil for deep-frying

3 cloves garlic, finely chopped

$1/4$ cup tomato sauce

2 tablespoons red wine vinegar

1 to 2 tablespoons fish sauce*

2 tablespoons sugar

$1/2$ teaspoon salt

4 to 6 red chile peppers, seeded and sliced (optional)

$1/2$ cup water

Garnish: Chinese parsley sprigs

Rinse fish well under running cold water. Score fish on both sides on the diagonal in a cross-hatch pattern every $3/4$ inch, cutting halfway to the bone. Coat fish lightly with 2 tablespoons of the cornstarch. Cut vegetables into 1- to 2-inch strips. Heat oil in a large wok on high heat until oil begins to get hot. Lower whole fish into the wok and reduce heat to medium. Cook for about 20 to 25 minutes, or until fish is cooked and crisp, being careful not to overcook. Set aside on a large platter. Heat 2 tablespoons of the oil and the garlic in a frying pan on medium heat until the garlic is golden brown. Stir in mixed vegetables, tomato sauce, red wine vinegar, fish sauce, sugar, salt and red chile peppers. Combine the remaining 2 tablespoons cornstarch and water; blend to make a smooth paste. Stir cornstarch mixture into sauce and cook 5 minutes, or until vegetables are cooked and sauce is thickened. Pour over fish and serve hot. Garnish with Chinese parsley.

*The amount of fish sauce used in the recipe depends on the brand selected and personal taste.

Whole Fish with Fresh Ginger and Yellow Bean Sauce

ILLUSTRATED ON PAGES 70 AND 71

Choose any seasonal red snapper, trout, catfish or other firm white fish. Deep-fry in a large wok. Serve with zesty Thai sauce and garnishes. A magnificent show-off entrée.

2 pounds whole fish

1 ounce dried Chinese black
   mushrooms

6 cups vegetable oil for deep-frying

2 cloves garlic, chopped

1/2 cup thinly sliced shallots

2 tablespoons shredded common ginger

2 tablespoons brown sugar

1 to 5 red chile peppers, seeded and
   chopped (optional)

1 tablespoon yellow bean sauce*

1 tablespoon oyster sauce

3 green onions, cut into 2-inch lengths

1 tablespoon cornstarch

1/2 cup cold water

3 tablespoons rice flour

3 cups chopped cabbage

Garnish: Red chile peppers

Chinese parsley sprigs, cut into
   2-inch lengths

Rinse fish well under running cold water. Score fish on both sides on the diagonal in a cross-hatch pattern every 3/4 inch, cutting halfway to the bone. Soak Chinese black mushrooms in warm water for 15 minutes; drain and discard stems. Cut caps into strips. In a saucepan heat 3 tablespoons of the oil. Add mushrooms, garlic and shallots and cook on medium heat, until golden brown. Add ginger, brown sugar, red chile peppers, yellow bean sauce, oyster sauce and green onions; mix well. Dissolve cornstarch in cold water and add to sauce; stir well. Reduce heat and simmer until sauce is thick. Pat fish dry with absorbent paper towels. In a large wok heat remaining oil for deep-frying on high heat for about 4 minutes. Coat fish with rice flour. Carefully place fish in oil, then immediately lower heat to medium. Fry fish until golden brown, about 10 to 15 minutes, depending on the thickness of the fish. Drain fish on absorbent paper towels to remove excess oil. Place chopped cabbage on a large platter and top with fish and pour on sauce. Garnish with red chile peppers and Chinese parsley.

*Yellow bean sauce from Thailand is saltier than sauce from Hong Kong or China. Season to taste.

MAKES 4 TO 6 SERVINGS

Opakapaka with Red Curry Sauce

Any firm white fish substitutes well in this recipe for crisp fried whole fish. Thai gourmets like it extra crispy. Catfish or mudfish are the favorites selected by Thai chefs for this dish.

2 pounds whole opakapaka (or any firm white fish)

2 tablespoons cornstarch

Vegetable oil for deep-frying, plus $1/4$ cup

$1/2$ small head cabbage, chopped

3 tablespoons Red Curry Paste (recipe page 126)

1 cup coconut milk

2 to 4 tablespoons fish sauce*

10 to 15 sweet basil leaves

Clean fish. Score fish on both sides on the diagonal in a crosshatch pattern every $3/4$ inch, cutting halfway to the bone. Coat fish lightly with the cornstarch. Heat oil for deep-frying to 350°F. Fry fish for 10 to 15 minutes, or until fish is cooked and crisp, being careful not to over-cook. Line a serving platter with chopped cabbage and place fish on top. Set aside. Heat the $1/4$ cup oil on medium-high heat and sauté red curry paste for 3 minutes. Stir in coconut milk and cook for 2 minutes. Reduce heat to medium-low; stir in fish sauce and basil. Cook for 3 minutes. Pour over fish.

*The amount of fish sauce used in the recipe depends on the brand selected and personal taste.

MAKES 3 TO 4 SERVINGS

Crab Legs with Yellow Bean Sauce

ILLUSTRATED ON PAGES 74 AND 75

Almost all seafood restaurants in Thailand serve a version of this crab leg dish with yellow bean sauce and green onions. A mild but colorful dish.

2 pounds crab legs

1 teaspoon cornstarch

$^1/_4$ cup cold water

$^1/_4$ cup vegetable oil

2 cloves garlic, chopped

$^1/_2$ onion, thinly sliced

1 egg, lightly beaten

1 tablespoon yellow bean sauce*

1 tablespoon oyster sauce

3 green onions, cut into 2-inch lengths

Garnish: Green onion brushes (directions page 183)

Rinse crab legs and cut into 2- to 3-inch lengths; crack shells. Combine cornstarch and cold water; stir to dissolve. In a wok heat oil, garlic and onion on high heat until garlic browns. Stir in egg; mix well. Add crab, yellow bean sauce, oyster sauce and cornstarch mixture. Reduce heat to medium and cook for 10 to 15 minutes, or until crab is cooked. Be careful not to overcook crab. Stir in green onions. Garnish with green onion brush. Serve hot.

Yellow bean sauce from Thailand is saltier than sauce from Hong Kong or China. Season to taste.

MAKES 4 SERVINGS

Lobster with Pineapple

In Thailand lobster tails are usually not served whole, but rather cut into bite-size pieces before cooking. This is a very unusual dish, but delicious!

4 lobster tails (6 ounces each)

1/4 cup vegetable oil

3 cloves garlic, chopped

1 stalk fresh lemongrass, finely chopped

1 teaspoon Red Curry Paste (recipe page 126)

1 egg, lightly beaten

1/2 cup water

1 cup pineapple chunks

2 to 4 tablespoons fish sauce*

1/2 teaspoon brown sugar

15 to 20 sweet basil leaves

Slit underside of lobster and press lightly to open. In a skillet heat oil on high heat; add garlic, lemongrass and red curry paste and cook until sauce bubbles. Stir in egg and cook for 1 minute. Add lobster and water and bring to a boil. Reduce heat to medium and add pineapple, fish sauce and brown sugar. Cook for 5 to 10 minutes, or until lobster is cooked, but not over-cooked. Stir in sweet basil. Serve immediately.

The amount of fish sauce used in the recipe depends on the brand selected and personal taste.

MAKES 4 SERVINGS

Scallops with Fresh Basil

ILLUSTRATED ON PAGES 78 AND 79

Fresh basil is excellent for stir-frying with seafood with poultry. Add a touch of garlic.

$1/2$ pound fresh scallops

2 tablespoons vegetable oil

3 cloves garlic, peeled and chopped

3 kaffir lime leaves, cut in thin strips

$1/2$ cup mushrooms (preferably straw mushrooms)

$1/4$ cup shredded bamboo shoots

3 tablespoons oyster sauce

2 to 4 red chile peppers, seeded and chopped (optional)

15 sweet basil leaves

2 cups chopped cabbage (optional)

Rinse scallops and score crosswise. In a wok heat oil, garlic and kaffir lime leaves on high heat, until oil bubbles. Add scallops, mushrooms, bamboo shoots, oyster sauce and red chile peppers; stir-fry for 5 minutes, or until scallops are cooked. Mix in basil and serve on a bed of chopped cabbage.

Note: The picture of this recipe is highly stylized. The version that you prepare will probably be more blended.

MAKES 2 TO 4 SERVINGS

Shrimp with Mixed Vegetables

Shrimp with Mixed Vegetables is very easy to prepare and takes only minutes to cook. Serve immediately after cooking for the freshest taste and appearance.

$1/2$ pound bay shrimp

2 tablespoons vegetable oil

2 cloves garlic, minced

$1/2$ pound mixed vegetables*

3 to 4 tablespoons oyster sauce

Rinse shrimp and pat dry. In a skillet heat oil; add garlic and cook until light brown. Stir in shrimp and cook 1 to 2 minutes, stirring constantly. Stir in mixed vegetables and oyster sauce and cook for 3 minutes.

Select from the following vegetables: bell peppers, string beans, water chestnuts, tomatoes, bamboo shoots, young corn, asparagus, cucumbers, zucchini, mushrooms, tofu

MAKES 4 SERVINGS

Fried Mussels with Fresh Whole Chile Peppers

ILLUSTRATED ON PAGE 82

Thai beaches are full of eateries and sidewalk food peddlers. Fried mussels are one of the favorite dishes for beachgoers.

$1/2$ pound mussels without shells

$1/4$ cup vegetable oil

4 cloves garlic, finely chopped

4 shallots, finely chopped

1 to 3 teaspoons yellow bean sauce*

10 to 20 small red chile peppers

1 tablespoon cornstarch

$1/4$ cup cold water

Garnish: Chinese parsley sprigs, cut into 2-inch lengths

Rinse mussels and pat dry on paper towels. In a wok heat oil on high heat with garlic and shallots until golden brown. Add mussels, yellow bean sauce and red chile peppers; stir-fry for 7 to 10 minutes. Dissolve cornstarch in cold water and stir into sauce in wok. Stir until sauce thickens. Garnish with Chinese parsley.

Yellow bean sauce from Thailand is saltier than sauce from Hong Kong or China. Season to taste.

MAKES 2 TO 4 SERVINGS

Honey Glazed Spareribs

This is one of the most popular items on our restaurant menu. Baby spareribs marinated in our homemade sauce, then grilled over a hot fire—simple and delicious.

4 pounds baby spareribs

4 stalks lemongrass, chopped

$1/2$ cup chopped garlic

3 tablespoons coarsely chopped fresh ginger

$1/2$ cup coarsely chopped Chinese parsley roots

$1/2$ cup honey

$1/2$ cup coconut milk

$1/4$ cup soy sauce

1 teaspoon salt

Sriracha sauce or sweet chile sauce for dipping

Garnish: Red chile pepper, sliced

Chinese parsley sprigs

Cut spareribs into individual ribs. In a food processor, combine lemongrass, garlic, ginger, Chinese parsley roots, honey, coconut milk, soy sauce, and salt; blend until smooth. Pour sauce over ribs and marinate overnight in the refrigerator. Preheat oven to 350°F. Place ribs in an open pan and bake for 1 hour, or until cooked, depending on the thickness of the ribs. Serve with Sriracha sauce for dipping. Garnish with red chile pepper and Chinese parsley sprigs.

Note: Another ideal method of cooking these ribs is grilled over hot charcoal.

MAKES 4 TO 6 SERVINGS

Pork Chops with Lemongrass and Garlic

ILLUSTRATED ON OPPOSITE PAGE

Lemongrass, garlic, soy sauce, and Chinese parsley roots make these pork chops very flavorful and aromatic.

2 pounds pork chops, $^3/_4$ inch thick

3 stalks lemongrass, chopped

$^1/_4$ cup chopped garlic

$^1/_4$ cup chopped Chinese parsley roots

3 tablespoons soy sauce

1 tablespoon brown sugar

$^1/_2$ teaspoon ground black pepper

$^1/_2$ cup vegetable oil

Sliced cabbage

Sticky rice or hot steamed rice

Garnish: Chinese parsley sprigs

Cucumber slices

Red chile peppers (optional)

In a bowl combine pork chops with lemongrass, garlic, Chinese parsley roots, soy sauce, brown sugar, and black pepper; toss lightly to coat. Cover and marinate in the refrigerator overnight. In a frying pan heat the oil to medium heat. Remove pork chops from marinade and fry for 10 to 12 minutes, or until cooked. Line a serving platter with cabbage and top with pork chops. Cook the marinade in the hot oil for 1 minute, or until brown, then pour over pork chops. Accompany with sticky rice or hot steamed rice. Garnish with Chinese parsley sprigs, cucumber slices, and red chile peppers.

MAKES 4 SERVINGS

Chicken with Fresh Sweet Basil

This original Thai dish, with basil, garlic, and chile peppers, is an excellent introduction to Thai cuisine. Most Thais prefer hot basil, which has a much stronger taste than the milder sweet basil.

1/2 pound boneless chicken breasts

2 tablespoons vegetable oil

3 cloves garlic, chopped

3 kaffir lime leaves, cut into thin strips

1/2 cup mushrooms (preferably straw mushrooms)

1/4 cup shredded bamboo shoots

3 tablespoons oyster sauce

2 to 4 red chile peppers, seeded and chopped (optional)

15 sweet basil leaves

2 cups chopped cabbage (optional)

Thinly cut chicken into 2-inch strips. In a wok heat oil, garlic and kaffir lime leaves on high heat, until the oil bubbles. Add chicken, mushrooms, bamboo shoots, oyster sauce and red chile peppers; stir-fry for 5 minutes, or until chicken is cooked. Mix in basil and serve on a bed of chopped cabbage.

MAKES 2 TO 4 SERVINGS

Bar-B-Que Chicken

Barbecued chicken is so popular in Thailand it is served almost everywhere…from portable food stations, bus stops, stadiums, to beaches.

2 whole young chickens

4 stalks fresh lemongrass

1 tablespoon coarsely chopped fresh ginger

1 ounce garlic, finely chopped (about 6 large cloves)

4 shallots

$^1/_2$ cup coarsely chopped Chinese parsley roots

3 tablespoons brown sugar

$^1/_2$ cup coconut milk

1 to 2 tablespoons fish sauce*

2 tablespoons soy sauce

2 tablespoons vegetable oil

Sticky rice (recipe page 148)

Garnish: Chinese parsley sprigs, cut into 2-inch lengths
Red chile peppers (optional)

Rinse chickens and pat dry. Split chickens down the breast, but do not cut all the way through; press open. Place chickens in a large bowl. In a food processor or blender combine lemongrass, ginger, garlic, shallots, parsley roots, brown sugar, coconut milk, fish sauce, soy sauce and oil; blend until smooth. Pour sauce over chickens and marinate overnight in the refrigerator. Preheat oven to 350°F. Place chickens on a rack in an open pan, with the split side down. Bake for about 1 hour, depending on the thickness of the chicken, or until the juices run clear when the thigh is pierced with a sharp knife. Serve with hot sticky rice. Garnish with Chinese parsley and red chile peppers.

*The amount of fish sauce used in this recipe depends on the brand selected and personal taste.

MAKES 4 TO 6 SERVINGS

Evil Jungle Prince with Chicken

ILLUSTRATED ON PAGES 90 AND 91

This spicy-flavored dish has quite a reputation for its unique name (developed by Keo himself in 1977 for his Mekong restaurant), and has been mentioned in such publications as Bon Appetit, Food and Wine, Bazaar, *and the* New York *and* Los Angeles Times. *Fresh basil, coconut milk, and red chile form a flavor for the gourmet's delight.*

$^1/_2$ pound boneless chicken breasts

2 to 6 small red chile peppers

$^1/_2$ stalk fresh lemongrass

2 kaffir lime leaves

2 tablespoons vegetable oil

$^1/_2$ cup coconut milk

$^1/_2$ teaspoon salt

1 to 3 tablespoons fish sauce*

10 to 15 sweet basil leaves

1 cup chopped cabbage

Thinly cut chicken into 2-inch strips. Grind together red chile peppers, lemongrass and kaffir limes leaves in a food processor or pound in a mortar. Heat oil to medium-high and sauté pepper mixture for 3 minutes. Stir in coconut milk and cook for 2 minutes. Add chicken and cook for 5 minutes, or until cooked. Reduce heat to medium-low. Stir in fish sauce and basil. Serve on bed of chopped cabbage.

The amount of fish sauce used in this recipe depends on the brand selected and personal taste.

MAKES 3 TO 4 SERVINGS

Thai Roast Duck

Duck is not used as much in Thai cooking as in Chinese.

    1 duck, about 3 pounds

    2 to 4 red chile peppers, seeded and finely chopped

    1 teaspoon Chinese five-spice powder

    1 tablespoon brown sugar

    1 teaspoon honey

    1 teaspoon lemon juice

    $^1/_2$ teaspoon salt

    $^1/_2$ teaspoon grated common ginger

    1 teaspoon soy sauce

    1 teaspoon sesame vegetable oil

    2 cloves garlic

Rinse duck and pat dry. Combine all the remaining ingredients in a food processor or blender; blend until smooth. Rub mixture all over and inside the duck. Preheat oven to 375°F. Place a wire rack in a shallow roasting pan; add a little water to the pan to reduce spattering of fat during cooking. Place duck on the rack. Bake for 1 hour, or until duck is cooked.

MAKES 4 TO 6 SERVINGS

Eggplant with Chicken

ILLUSTRATED ON OPPOSITE PAGE

A gourmet delight, yet amazingly easy.

$3/4$ pound Japanese eggplant (about 3 cups sliced)

$1/3$ pound boneless chicken breast

6 tablespoons vegetable oil

2 to 3 cloves garlic, chopped

1 to 5 red chile peppers, seeded and chopped

10 to 15 sweet basil leaves

1 to 3 tablespoons yellow bean sauce*

Slice unpeeled eggplant crosswise into slices $1/8$ inch thick. Thinly slice chicken. Heat oil in a wok; add garlic and stir-fry until light brown. Add eggplant and chicken and cook for 5 to 7 minutes. Add red chile peppers, basil leaves and yellow bean sauce; mix well. Serve immediately, since eggplant and basil turn dark if dish sits after cooking.

Yellow bean sauce from Thailand is saltier than sauce from Hong Kong or China. Season to taste.

MAKES 3 TO 4 SERVINGS

Roast Duck with Chile

Roast duck pieces stir-fried with red dried chile peppers, garlic and shallots makes a very spicy and delicious dish. This is a favorite among the "Chinese Thais" in Bangkok.

1 roast duck

$^1/_4$ cup vegetable oil

8 cloves garlic, chopped

10 shallots, chopped

1 stalk fresh lemongrass, finely chopped

1 ounce Chinese parsley roots, chopped

1 teaspoon cornstarch

$^1/_4$ cup cold water

20 to 30 large dried red chile peppers, soaked, drained, and seeded

2 to 4 tablespoons fish sauce*

1 teaspoon soy sauce

2 to 3 tablespoons brown sugar or honey

Garnish: Chinese parsley sprigs

Cut duck into serving pieces. In a skillet heat oil; add garlic, shallots, lemongrass and Chinese parsley roots and cook until light brown. Combine cornstarch and water; blend to make a smooth paste. Stir duck, red chile peppers, fish sauce, soy sauce, cornstarch mixture and brown sugar into duck. Reduce heat to medium and cook for 10 minutes. Garnish with Chinese parsley. Serve with hot steamed rice.

*The amount of fish sauce used in this recipe depends on the brand selected and personal taste.

Makes 4 to 6 servings

Chicken with Black Mushrooms

Many people believe this dish originated in China. Chinese influence in Thai and other Southeast Asian cuisine is undeniable, however, they all have developed their own nuances.

1 pound boneless chicken breasts

10 large dried Chinese black mushrooms

$1/4$ cup vegetable oil

3 cloves garlic, chopped

4 shallots, chopped

$1/2$ ounce common ginger, shredded

1 teaspoon cornstarch

$1/4$ cup water

2 to 4 tablespoons fish sauce*

2 tablespoons brown sugar or honey

$1/4$ teaspoon salt

Garnish: Chinese parsley sprigs

1 green onion, cut into 2-inch lengths

3 red chile peppers, seeded and thinly sliced

Thinly cut chicken into 2-inch strips. Soak Chinese black mushrooms in warm water for 15 minutes; drain and discard stems. Slice mushrooms into 1-inch strips. In a skillet heat oil; add garlic, shallots and ginger and cook until light brown. Add chicken and stir-fry 2 to 3 minutes. Combine cornstarch and water; blend to make a smooth paste. Stir mushrooms, cornstarch mixture, fish sauce, brown sugar, and salt into chicken. Stir-fry for 2 minutes, then reduce heat to medium and cook for 10 minutes, or until chicken is cooked. Garnish with Chinese parsley, green onion and red chile peppers. Serve with hot steamed rice.

*The amount of fish sauce used in this recipe depends on the brand selected and personal taste.

MAKES 2 TO 3 SERVINGS

Cashew Chicken

ILLUSTRATED ON OPPOSITE PAGE

An easy, exotic dish of roasted cashew nuts stir-fried with tender slices of chicken, green onions, oyster sauce and a touch of garlic.

$3/4$ pound boneless chicken breasts

$1/4$ cup vegetable oil

2 cloves garlic, crushed

2 tablespoons oyster sauce

8 green onions, cut into 2-inch lengths

1 to 5 whole dried red chile peppers

$3/4$ pound unsalted roasted cashew nuts (about 3 cups)

4 large lettuce leaves

Garnish: Green onion brush (directions page 183)

Thinly slice chicken. Heat oil in a wok; add garlic and stir-fry until light brown. Add chicken and oyster sauce and cook for 4 to 6 minutes. Reduce heat to medium. Add green onions, red chile peppers and cashew nuts; mix well. Place lettuce leaves on a platter and top with chicken. Garnish with green onion brush.

MAKES 3 TO 4 SERVINGS

Beef with String Beans and Fresh Ginger

This spicy hot dish is made with all fresh ingredients. A delightfully different recipe.

$1/2$ pound beef

$1/2$ pound fresh string beans

2 tablespoons vegetable oil

1 stalk fresh lemongrass, finely chopped

1 tablespoon shredded common ginger

1 to 5 red chile peppers, seeded and finely chopped

$1/2$ cup coconut milk

$1/4$ teaspoon salt

3 cups chopped cabbage (optional)

Thinly slice beef into 2-inch strips. Cut string beans into 2-inch strips. Heat oil in a wok with lemongrass, ginger and red chile peppers on high heat, until oil bubbles. Add beef, coconut milk, string beans and salt; stir-fry for 3 minutes, or until beef is cooked. Serve on a bed of chopped cabbage.

MAKES 6 SERVINGS

Beef with Fresh Sweet Basil

Stir-fried beef with fresh sweet basil accompanied, of course, by steamed rice is to a Thai as meat and potatoes are to an American.

$1/2$ pound beef

2 tablespoons vegetable oil

3 cloves garlic, chopped

3 kaffir lime leaves, cut in thin strips

$1/2$ cup mushrooms (preferably straw mushrooms)

$1/4$ cup shredded bamboo shoots

3 tablespoons oyster sauce

2 to 4 red chile peppers, seeded and chopped (optional)

15 sweet basil leaves

2 cups chopped cabbage (optional)

Thinly cut beef into 2-inch strips. Heat oil in a wok with garlic and kaffir lime leaves on high heat, until oil bubbles. Add beef, mushrooms, bamboo shoots, oyster sauce and red chile peppers; stir-fry for 5 minutes, or until beef is cooked. Mix in basil and serve on a bed of chopped cabbage.

Makes 2 to 4 servings

Beef with Oyster Sauce

ILLUSTRATED ON PAGES 102 AND 103

This is a good recipe when you don't know exactly how many to expect for dinner. Just make extra. It's good the next day.

1 pound flank steak

1 ounce dried Chinese black mushrooms

2 tablespoons vegetable oil

2 cloves garlic, minced

3 tablespoons oyster sauce

Thinly slice flank steak on the diagonal into strips 1 inch wide by 2 to 3 inches in length. Soak Chinese black mushrooms in warm water for 15 minutes; drain and discard stems. Thinly slice mushroom caps. In a skillet heat oil; add garlic and cook until light brown. Stir in beef and cook 1 to 2 minutes, stirring constantly. Stir in mushrooms and cook for 1 minute. Add oyster sauce and cook for 1 minute.

MAKES 4 SERVINGS

Crispy Fried Beef

Crispy fried sun-dried beef is very popular in Northern Thailand and Laos. People love it with sticky rice and green papaya salad.

2 pounds flank steak

3 tablespoons finely chopped lemongrass

6 tablespoons chopped red chiles

5 tablespoons chopped garlic

5 tablespoons chopped Chinese parsley roots

$1/4$ cup chopped shallots

$1/2$ teaspoon chopped fresh ginger

$1/4$ cup fish sauce

2 tablespoons sugar

6 kaffir lime leaves, finely chopped

5 cups vegetable oil for deep-frying

Hot sticky rice

Sriracha sauce

Cut flank steak lengthwise, with the grain, into strips 1 to 2 inches wide and 5 to 6 inches long. In a mortar or food processor grind together lemongrass, chiles, garlic, Chinese parsley roots, shallots, and ginger. In a bowl or plastic bag, combine lemongrass mixture, fish sauce, sugar, and kaffir lime leaves. Add beef strips and mix well to coat. Refrigerate, covered, for 1 to 2 hours to allow beef to marinate. On a large cookie sheet lay out strips of beef and dry them in the hot sun for 1 to 2 days, or in the oven at the lowest heat, until dried, about 5 to 6 hours. In a wok, bring the oil to high heat. Fry beef piece by piece for 2 to 4 minutes, or until cooked. Remove from oil and place on absorbent paper towels. Serve with hot sticky rice and Sriracha sauce.

Note: Another method of cooking is to grill beef over charcoal.

MAKES 4 TO 6 SERVINGS

Vegetable Dishes

String Beans with Fresh Ginger

ILLUSTRATED ON OPPOSITE PAGE

This spicy hot vegetarian dish is made with all fresh ingredients. A delightfully different recipe.

$^1/_2$ pound fresh string beans

2 tablespoons vegetable oil

1 stalk fresh lemongrass, finely chopped

1 tablespoon shredded common ginger

1 to 5 red chile peppers, seeded and finely chopped

$^1/_2$ cup coconut milk

$^1/_4$ teaspoon salt

3 cups chopped cabbage

Cut string beans into 2-inch strips. Heat oil in a wok with lemongrass, ginger and red chile peppers until oil starts to bubble. Stir in coconut milk, string beans and salt; cook on high heat for 3 minutes. Serve on a bed of chopped cabbage.

MAKES 3 TO 4 SERVINGS

Eggplant with Tofu

A gourmet delight, yet amazingly easy.

$^3/_4$ pound Japanese eggplant (about 3 cups sliced)

$^1/_4$ pound tofu

6 tablespoons vegetable oil

2 to 3 cloves garlic, chopped

1 to 5 red chile peppers, seeded and chopped

10 to 15 sweet basil leaves

1 to 3 tablespoons yellow bean sauce*

Slice unpeeled eggplant crosswise into slices $^1/_8$ inch thick. Cut tofu into $^1/_2$-inch cubes. Heat oil in skillet; add garlic and stir-fry until light brown. Add eggplant and tofu and cook for 5 to 7 minutes. Add remaining ingredients; mix gently. Serve immediately, since eggplant and basil turn dark if dish sits after cooking.

Yellow bean sauce from Thailand is saltier than sauce from Hong Kong or China. Season to taste.

MAKES 3 TO 4 SERVINGS

Stir-Fried Ong Choi with Yellow Bean Sauce

Ong choi (Asian watercress) stir-fried with bean sauce or fish sauce is very popular in Thailand.

$^1/_4$ cup vegetable oil

3 cloves garlic, finely chopped

2 pounds ong choi, cut into 2-inch lengths

1 to 3 teaspoons yellow bean sauce*

2 teaspoons oyster sauce

3 to 5 red chile peppers, seeded and thinly sliced (optional)

Heat oil on high heat in a large wok with garlic until brown. Add ong choi, yellow bean sauce, oyster sauce, and red chile peppers; stir-fry for 2 minutes, or until the ong choi softens. Serve immediately, since ong choi darkens a few minutes after it is cooked.

Note: Broccoli, head cabbage, spinach or cauliflower can be substituted for the ong choi.

*Yellow bean sauce from Thailand is saltier than sauce from Hong Kong or China. Season to taste.

MAKES 3 TO 4 SERVINGS

Evil Jungle Prince with Mixed Vegetables

ILLUSTRATED ON OPPOSITE PAGE

The most popular vegetarian dish at all of Keo's restaurants.

$1/2$ pound mixed vegetables (refer to page 81)

6 small red chile peppers

$1/2$ stalk fresh lemongrass

2 kaffir lime leaves

2 tablespoons vegetable oil

$1/2$ cup coconut milk

$1/4$ teaspoon salt

10 to 15 sweet basil leaves

1 cup chopped cabbage

Cut vegetables into thin strips. Grind together red chile peppers, lemongrass and kaffir lime leaves in a food processor or pound in a mortar. Heat oil to medium-high and sauté pepper mixture for 3 minutes. Stir in coconut milk and cook for 2 minutes. Add vegetables and cook for 5 minutes. Reduce heat to medium-low. Stir in salt and basil. Serve on bed of chopped cabbage.

MAKES 3 TO 4 SERVINGS

Thai Sweet-and-Sour Vegetables

More vegetables! That's what makes this Thai sweet-and-sour dish so extra good and somewhat different than the Chinese version.

1 pound mixed vegetables (refer to page 81)

2 tablespoons vegetable oil

3 cloves garlic, finely chopped

1/4 cup tomato sauce

2 tablespoons red wine vinegar

1 to 2 tablespoons fish sauce*

2 tablespoons sugar

1/2 teaspoon salt

4 to 6 red chile peppers, seeded and sliced (optional)

2 tablespoons cornstarch

1/2 cup water

Cut vegetables into 1- to 2-inch strips. Heat oil and the garlic in a frying pan on medium heat until garlic is golden brown. Stir in mixed vegetables, tomato sauce, red wine vinegar, fish sauce, sugar, salt and red chile peppers. Combine the cornstarch and water; blend to make a smooth paste. Stir cornstarch mixture into sauce and cook 5 minutes, or until vegetables are cooked and sauce is thickened.

The amount of fish sauce used in the recipe depends on the brand selected and personal taste.

MAKES 3 TO 4 SERVINGS

Asparagus with Black Mushrooms

Asparagus is very popular among the Chinese Thai in Bangkok. This combination of asparagus and Chinese black mushrooms is really delicious and a very simple dish to prepare. Hot food lovers, add a few chile peppers.

1 pound fresh or canned asparagus

1 ounce dried Chinese black mushrooms

2 tablespoons vegetable oil

2 cloves garlic, minced

3 to 4 tablespoons oyster sauce

2 to 4 red chile peppers, seeded and sliced (optional)

Rinse asparagus; peel and trim ends. Soak Chinese black mushrooms in warm water for 15 minutes; drain and discard stems. Leave whole or slice into 1-inch strips. In a skillet heat oil; add garlic and cook until light brown. Stir in mushrooms and cook, stirring constantly, for 1 minute. Add asparagus, oyster sauce and red chile peppers; stir-fry for 3 minutes. Serve hot.

MAKES 3 TO 4 SERVINGS

Sauces and Pastes

Satay Sauce

ILLUSTRATED ON PAGE 118

Satay is an excellent dip for assorted chilled vegetables and meats.

$1/4$ cup vegetable oil

2 cloves garlic, minced

1 onion, chopped

$1/2$ to 1 teaspoon ground dried red chile peppers

3 kaffir lime leaves

$1/2$ teaspoon curry powder

1 tablespoon chopped fresh lemongrass

1 cup coconut milk

$1/2$ cup milk

1 2-inch cinnamon stick

3 bay leaves

2 teaspoons tamarind paste

1 to 3 tablespoons fish sauce*

3 tablespoons dark brown sugar

3 tablespoons lemon juice

1 cup chunky peanut butter

Heat oil in a skillet to medium-high heat and sauté garlic, onion, chile peppers, kaffir lime leaves, curry powder and lemongrass for 2 to 3 minutes. Stir in coconut milk, milk, cinnamon stick, bay leaves, tamarind paste, fish sauce, brown sugar, lemon juice and peanut butter; mix well. Reduce heat and cook, stirring frequently, until sauce thickens, about 30 minutes. Be very careful sauce does not stick to bottom of pan.

*The amount of fish sauce used in the recipe depends on the brand selected and personal taste.

MAKES 3 CUPS

Clockwise from top: Satay Sauce (page 119), Cucumber Sauce (page 121), and Spring Roll Sauce (page 120)

Spring Roll Sauce

ILLUSTRATED ON PAGE 118

Spring Roll Sauce can be used as a sauce for almost any deep-fried meat or vegetable dish.

$^1/_4$ cup sugar

$^1/_2$ cup water

$^1/_2$ cup red wine vinegar

1 to 2 tablespoons fish sauce*

2 to 3 teaspoons ground red chile peppers

$^1/_2$ carrot or daikon, shredded

$^1/_4$ cup coarsely chopped peanuts or macadamia nuts

In a small saucepan combine sugar and water; bring to a boil. Reduce heat and simmer for about 10 minutes, or until sugar is dissolved. Remove from heat. Stir in red wine vinegar, fish sauce and red chile peppers. Pour sauce into serving bowl. Chill, then top with carrots and sprinkle with peanuts before serving.

The amount of fish sauce used in the recipe depends on the brand selected and personal taste.

MAKES 1 CUP

Cucumber Sauce

ILLUSTRATED ON PAGE 118

Cucumber Sauce often accompanies satay dishes and fish patties.

1 cucumber (preferably Japanese)

5 tablespoons sugar

1 cup boiling water

$1/2$ cup white vinegar

1 teaspoon salt

3 to 5 red chile peppers, seeded and finely chopped

3 shallots, finely chopped

Garnish: 6 to 8 sprigs Chinese parsley

Thinly slice cucumber; arrange in a bowl. Dissolve sugar in boiling water; stir in white vinegar and salt. Pour sauce over cucumber slices. Sprinkle with chile peppers and shallots. Chill. Garnish with Chinese parsley.

MAKES 1 $1/2$ CUPS

Regular (Musamun) Curry Paste

ILLUSTRATED ON PAGE 122

Thai curry pastes are unique because they are always made with fresh leaves, roots and herbs. Whereas Indian curries depend upon dry ingredients. This is a Thai version of a Moslem curry, rich in spices but quite mild and a little sweet.

20 to 30 large dried chile peppers, seeded

1 stalk fresh lemongrass, coarsely chopped

1 cup thinly sliced shallots

5 cloves garlic

1 tablespoon coarsely chopped kra chai

10 fresh kaffir lime leaves, chopped

1 tablespoon Chinese parsley root

1 tablespoon Chinese parsley seeds or coriander seeds

1 teaspoon cumin seeds

1 teaspoon salt

$^1/_2$ teaspoon ground cinnamon

1 teaspoon brown sugar

$^1/_4$ teaspoon shrimp paste (optional)

2 tablespoons vegetable oil

Soak dried red chile peppers in water for 5 minutes, or; drain. Combine all the ingredients in a 2-inch–deep pan and bake at 350°F for 15 to 20 minutes. Then process in a food processor until smooth. If a mortar and pestle are used, then add oil after all other ingredients are ground. Refrigerate in a glass container. Paste keeps well for several months.

Top row from left: Regular (Musamun) Curry Sauce, Yellow Curry Sauce, Red Curry Sauce, and Green Curry Sauce

Bottom row from left: Regular (Musamun) Curry Paste (page 124), Yellow Curry Paste (page 125), Red Curry Paste (page 126), and Green Curry Paste (page 127)

Yellow Curry Paste

ILLUSTRATED ON PAGE 122

Yellow curry is Americans' favorite in Thailand. It is the mildest of all the curries.

5 to 10 fresh yellow chile peppers, seeded

1 stalk fresh lemongrass, coarsely chopped

$1/4$ cup thinly sliced shallots

2 tablespoons coarsely chopped garlic

1 teaspoon coarsely chopped kra-chai

1 teaspoon coriander seeds

1 teaspoon caraway seeds

1 teaspoon curry powder

1 teaspoon dried mustard

1 teaspoon salt

$1/2$ teaspoon ground cinnamon

1 tablespoon sugar

2 tablespoons vegetable oil

Combine all the ingredients in a food processor and process until smooth. If a mortar and pestle is used, then add oil after all other ingredients are ground. Refrigerate in a glass container. Paste keeps well for several months.

Red Curry Paste

ILLUSTRATED ON PAGES 122 AND 123

The original Thai curry.

15 to 20 red chile peppers, seeded

2 stalks fresh lemongrass, coarsely chopped

5 shallots, thinly sliced

1 clove garlic

1 tablespoons coarsely chopped kha

3 kaffir lime leaves, chopped

$1/4$ cup Chinese parsley roots

$1/2$ teaspoon ground coriander

$1/2$ teaspoon ground caraway seeds

$1/2$ to 1 tablespoons fish sauce,* or 1 teaspoon salt

$1/4$ teaspoon shrimp paste (optional)

2 tablespoons vegetable oil

Combine all the ingredients in a food processor and process until smooth. If a mortar and pestle is used, then add oil after all other ingredients are ground. Refrigerate in a glass container. Paste keeps well for several months.

The amount of fish sauce used in this recipe depends on the brand selected and personal taste.

Green Curry Paste

ILLUSTRATED ON PAGE 123

Another original Thai creation…the hottest among all Thai curries.

15 to 20 fresh small Thai green chile peppers

4 stalks fresh lemongrass, coarsely chopped

3 shallots, thinly sliced

1 clove garlic

1 tablespoon coarsely chopped kha

1 tablespoon coarsely chopped kra-chai

5 kaffir lime leaves, chopped

1/2 teaspoon chopped kaffir lime rind

1/2 teaspoon ground coriander

1/2 teaspoon ground caraway seeds

1/2 to 1 tablespoon fish sauce*

1 tablespoon sugar

1/4 teaspoon shrimp paste (optional)

2 tablespoons vegetable oil

Combine all the ingredients in a food processor and process until smooth. If a mortar and pestle is used, then add oil after all other ingredients are ground. Refrigerate in a glass container. Paste keeps well for several months.

The amount of fish sauce used in this recipe depends on the brand selected and personal taste.

Thai Curry Sauce

Thai curry sauces are made by adding coconut milk to the curry paste. Remember! Amount of paste determines how hot and spicy your sauce will be.

2 tablespoons vegetable oil

1 teaspoon red, green, yellow or regular curry paste

1 cup coconut milk

Heat oil in a saucepan on high heat. Add curry paste of your choice and stir-fry for 1 to 2 minutes; add coconut milk. Bring mixture to a boil, then remove from heat immediately.

Curries

Musamun Beef Curry

ILLUSTRATED ON OPPOSITE PAGE

Beef chunks sautéed in Thai curry with potatoes and coconut milk, then cooked at low heat to perfection—a favorite of Americans in Thailand.

$^{1}/_{2}$ pound beef

2 tablespoons vegetable oil

1 teaspoon Regular (Musamun) Curry Paste (recipe page 124)

1 potato, peeled and cut into 1-inch cubes

1 onion, quartered

1 cup coconut milk

1 to 2 tablespoons fish sauce*

1 teaspoon brown sugar

1 to 5 red chile peppers, chopped (optional)

$^{1}/_{2}$ cup roasted peanuts

Hot steamed rice

Cut beef into 1-inch cubes. In a saucepan heat oil and regular curry paste on high heat, until curry paste bubbles. Add beef, potato, onion, coconut milk, fish sauce, brown sugar and red chile peppers; stir well and cook for about 10 minutes. Reduce heat and simmer for 30 minutes. Serve immediately. Sprinkle with roasted peanuts. Accompany with hot steamed rice.

Note: Lamb can be substituted for beef.

*The amount of fish sauce used in this recipe depends on the brand selected and personal taste.

MAKES 4 SERVINGS

Top: Musamun Beef Curry (page 131)
Bottom: Yellow Chicken Curry (page 132)

Yellow Chicken Curry

ILLUSTRATED ON PAGE 130

Yellow curry is the mildest of all Thai curries. It goes best with chicken or seafood.

$^1/_2$ pound boneless chicken breasts

2 potatoes, peeled

2 tablespoons vegetable oil

1 teaspoon Yellow Curry Paste (recipe page 125)

1 cup coconut milk

2 tablespoons fish sauce

1 teaspoon brown sugar

1 to 5 yellow chile peppers, seeded and chopped (optional)

Hot steamed rice

Thinly slice chicken into 2-inch strips. Cut potatoes into 1-inch cubes. In a saucepan heat oil and curry paste on high heat, until curry paste bubbles. Add chicken, potatoes, coconut milk, fish sauce, brown sugar and yellow chile peppers; stir well and cook for about 7 minutes, or until chicken is cooked. Serve immediately. Accompany with hot steamed rice.

Note: Any combination of seafood can be substituted for the chicken.

MAKES 4 SERVINGS

Thai Crab Curry

An elegant blend of seafood and yellow curry...perfect for guests.

2 pounds cooked king crab

1/4 cup vegetable oil

2 teaspoons Yellow Curry Paste (recipe page 125)

2 cups coconut milk

2 to 4 tablespoons fish sauce*

2 teaspoons brown sugar or honey

1 to 5 yellow chile peppers, seeded and chopped (optional)

3 green onions, cut into 2-inch lengths

Hot steamed rice

Cut king crab into serving pieces. Leave shell on, but crack shell on each piece. In a saucepan heat oil and yellow curry paste on high heat, until curry paste bubbles. Add crab, coconut milk, fish sauce, brown sugar and yellow chile peppers; stir well and cook for about 7 minutes, or until crab is heated through. Stir in green onions. Serve immediately. Accompany with hot steamed rice.

The amount of fish sauce used in this recipe depends on the brand selected and personal taste.

MAKES 6 SERVINGS

Red Pork Curry

Fresh red chile peppers give this curry dish its heat, its flavor and its name.

$^1/_2$ pound lean pork

2 tablespoons vegetable oil

1 teaspoon Red Curry Paste (recipe page 126)

$^1/_2$ cup shredded young bamboo shoots

3 kaffir lime leaves

1 cup coconut milk

10 to 15 sweet basil leaves

1 to 2 tablespoons fish sauce*

1 to 5 red chile peppers, chopped (optional)

Garnish: Red chile peppers

Kaffir lime leaves

Sweet basil leaves (optional)

Hot steamed rice

Cut pork into thin strips. In a saucepan heat oil and red curry paste on high heat, until curry paste bubbles. Add pork, bamboo shoots, kaffir lime leaves and coconut milk; stir well and cook for about 10 minutes, or until pork is cooked. Mix in basil, fish sauce and red chile peppers. Garnish with red chile peppers, kaffir lime leaves and basil leaves. Serve immediately. Accompany with hot steamed rice.

Idea: An excellent vegetarian curry can be prepared by substituting mixed vegetables for the pork. Use $^1/_2$ teaspoon salt instead of the fish sauce.

*The amount of fish sauce used in this recipe depends on the brand selected and personal taste.

MAKES 4 SERVINGS

Left: Red Pork Curry (page 135)
Right: Green Shrimp Curry (page 136)

Green Shrimp Curry

ILLUSTRATED ON PAGE 134

Eggplant, shrimp and coconut milk makes a nice combination. It's the green curry that makes it Thai's hottest!

$^1/_2$ pound fresh large shrimp

2 tablespoons vegetable oil

1 teaspoon Green Curry Paste (recipe page 127)

1 cup Thai eggplant

3 kaffir lime leaves

1 stalk fresh lemongrass, thinly sliced

1 cup coconut milk

10 to 15 sweet basil leaves

1 to 2 tablespoons fish sauce*

1 to 5 small green chile peppers, seeded and chopped (optional)

Garnish: Kaffir lime leaves

Slices fresh lemongrass

Sweet basil leaves (optional)

Hot steamed rice

Rinse shrimp and devein. In a saucepan heat oil and green curry paste on high heat, until curry paste bubbles. Add shrimp, eggplant, kaffir lime leaves, lemongrass and coconut milk; stir well and cook for about 7 minutes, or until shrimp are cooked. Mix in basil, fish sauce and green chile peppers. Garnish with kaffir lime leaves, sliced fresh lemongrass and basil leaves. Serve immediately. Accompany with hot steamed rice.

Note: Green peas can be substituted for Thai eggplant. Chicken can be substituted for the shrimp.

*The amount of fish sauce used in this recipe depends on the brand selected and personal taste.

MAKES 6 SERVINGS

Panang Duck Curry

ILLUSTRATED ON PAGES 138 AND 139

This thick, dark, red curry with peanut butter is a flavorful combination with roast duck.

1 roast duck

2 tablespoons vegetable oil

1 teaspoon Regular (Musamun) Curry Paste (recipe page 124)

1 cup small Thai eggplant

3 kaffir lime leaves

1 cup coconut milk

1 tablespoon brown sugar

2 tablespoons peanut butter

Garnish: Kaffir lime leaves (optional)

Hot steamed rice

Cut duck into serving pieces. In a saucepan heat oil and regular curry paste on high heat, until curry paste bubbles. Add duck, eggplant, kaffir lime leaves, coconut milk, brown sugar and peanut butter; stir well and cook for about 7 minutes, or until heated through. Garnish with kaffir lime leaves. Serve immediately. Accompany with hot steamed rice.

Note: Green peas can be substituted for the Thai eggplant. Chicken or beef can be substituted for the roast duck.

MAKES 6 SERVINGS

Rice and Noodles

Thai Noodles with Chicken

ILLUSTRATED ON OPPOSITE PAGE

One of the favorite dishes of Americans in Thailand. It is sold everywhere from fine dining restaurants to sidewalk food stands.

$1/2$ pound rice noodles

$1/4$ cup vegetable oil

2 cloves garlic, finely chopped

1 scant teaspoon shredded pickled salted radish

$1/4$ pound boneless chicken breast, sliced

1 egg, lightly beaten

$1/2$ pound bean sprouts

1 tablespoon catsup

1 teaspoon soy sauce

$1/4$ cup coarsely chopped peanuts or macadamia nuts

1 teaspoon sugar

1 to 2 tablespoons fish sauce*

1 tablespoon dried ground salted shrimp (optional)

1 ounce chives, cut into 2-inch lengths

Garnish: Chives

1 lime, quartered

1 teaspoon dried red chile pepper flakes (optional)

Soak rice noodles in warm water for 30 minutes; drain. Heat oil in a wok on high heat and cook garlic and salted radish until light brown. Add chicken and egg; stir-fry for 3 to 4 minutes. Add rice noodles and half of the bean sprouts; mix well. Stir in catsup, soy sauce, peanuts, sugar, fish sauce and ground salted shrimp; cook for 3 minutes. Add chives and the remaining bean sprouts; mix well. Serve hot. Garnish with chives, lime quarters and red chile pepper flakes. Sprinkle with extra chopped peanuts, if desired.

*The amount of fish sauce used in this recipe depends on the brand selected and personal taste.

MAKES 3 TO 4 SERVINGS

Fried Noodles with Shrimp

This spicier version of Singapore noodles is quick and easy to prepare.

1 ounce rice noodles

$1/4$ cup vegetable oil

3 cloves garlic, chopped

6 shallots, chopped

$1/4$ pound fresh large shrimp, peeled and deveined

1 onion, thinly sliced

1 egg, lightly beaten

2 to 3 tablespoons fish sauce*

1 ounce chives, cut into 2-inch lengths

$1/4$ teaspoon ground dried chile peppers (optional)

3 ounces bean sprouts

Garnish: Chinese parsley sprigs

3 red chile peppers, thinly sliced

1 lime, quartered

Soak rice noodles in warm water for 15 minutes; drain and cut into 4-inch lengths. In a skillet heat oil; add garlic and shallots and cook until light brown. Stir in shrimp, onion and egg and stir-fry for 2 minutes, then reduce heat to medium. Stir in rice noodles, fish sauce, chives and ground dried chile peppers. Add bean sprouts; mix well and cook for 2 minutes. Serve immediately. Garnish with Chinese parsley, red chile peppers and lime.

The amount of fish sauce used in this recipe depends on the brand selected and personal taste.

Makes 2 to 4 servings

Pineapple Fried Rice with Dried Shrimp

There are many variations of Thai fried rice. It's not as dry as Chinese fried rice. Because of its ingredients, Thai fried rice is moist and flaky.

1 tablespoon vegetable oil

1 onion, chopped

$1/4$ cup chopped shallots

6 cloves garlic, chopped

2 eggs, lightly beaten

4 cups cooked steamed jasmine rice

1 cup sliced pineapple

2 to 3 tablespoons fish sauce

$1/2$ cup dried shrimp or cooked chicken

$1/2$ cup peas

Garnish: 3 tablespoons thinly sliced green onion

2 to 3 fresh red chile peppers, sliced (optional)

3 tablespoons chopped Chinese parsley

In a wok or frying pan, heat the oil on medium heat until the oil is hot. Add onion, shallots, and garlic and stir-fry for 1 to 2 minutes, or until the mixture is light brown. Add eggs and immediately add the rice, pineapple, fish sauce, dried shrimp, and peas. Stir-fry for 2 minutes, or until the ingredients are evenly mixed. Garnish with green onion, red chile peppers, and Chinese parsley before serving.

MAKES 4 TO 6 SERVINGS

Thai Broccoli Noodles with Shrimp

ILLUSTRATED ON OPPOSITE PAGE

Shrimp with Asian broccoli and yellow bean sauce make this a good everyday dish.

$1/_2$ pound shrimp

4 tablespoons vegetable oil

$1/_2$ pound fresh wide rice noodles

2 eggs (optional)

3 cloves garlic, finely chopped

1 pound broccoli (preferably Asian), cut into 2-inch lengths

1 to 3 teaspoons yellow bean sauce*

2 teaspoons oyster sauce

Peel and devein shrimp, leaving tails on for color. Heat 2 tablespoons of the oil in a large wok on medium heat. Add rice noodles and eggs; mix well and cook for 2 minutes. Place rice noodles on a large serving platter; set aside. Heat the remaining 2 tablespoons of the oil on high heat in the same wok with garlic, until garlic is golden brown. Add shrimp, broccoli, yellow bean sauce and oyster sauce. Stir-fry for 2 to 3 minutes. Add noodles and toss lightly. Serve immediately.

Idea: Tofu, meat, or other seafood can be substituted in this recipe.

*Yellow bean sauce from Thailand is saltier than sauce from Hong Kong or China. Season to taste.

Makes 2 to 4 servings

Brown Rice

2^1/$_2$ cups brown rice

3 cups water

Salt to taste

Rinse rice in a colander until water runs clear; drain well. In a heavy saucepan with a tight fitting lid bring water and rice to a boil. Stir continuously until bubbles disappear from surface. Remove any scum. Continue boiling until there is only a thin film of water covering the rice. Reduce heat to a simmer and cover with the lid. Cook for 10 to 15 minutes, or until rice is tender. Remove from heat and fluff rice with a spatula. Cover for 5 more minutes. Serve hot.

MAKES 4 TO 4^1/$_2$ CUPS

Steamed Rice

2^1/$_2$ cups long grain rice

3 cups water

Salt to taste

Rinse rice in a colander until water runs clear; drain well. In a heavy saucepan with a tight fitting lid bring water and rice to a boil. Stir continuously until bubbles disappear from surface. Remove any scum. Continue boiling until there is only a thin film of water covering the rice. Reduce heat to a simmer and cover with the lid. Cook for 10 to 15 minutes, or until rice is tender. Remove from heat and fluff rice with a spatula. Cover for 5 more minutes. Serve hot.

MAKES 4 TO 4^1/$_2$ CUPS

Sticky Rice

1 cup sticky rice

Rinse rice in a colander until water runs clear; drain well. Place rice in a bowl and add water to cover. Let stand 12 hours or overnight. Drain. Spread rice in an even layer in a steamer lined with cheesecloth or in a sticky rice steaming basket. Cook, covered, over boiling water for 40 to 45 minutes, or until tender and translucent. Remove from heat and fluff rice with a spatula. Serve hot.

MAKES 1^1/$_2$ CUPS

Water Chestnut Fried Rice

ILLUSTRATED ON PAGE 150

Like Thai noodles, Thai-style fried rice is served at any meal or as a snack. City folks like it better than villagers, however. A perfect dish for those who are vegetarians. The addition of pineapple chunks and shredded carrots give the dish color and a sweet-sour taste.

2 tablespoons vegetable oil

1 clove garlic, finely chopped

1 onion, thinly sliced

3 cups cooked rice

1 can (6 oz.) sliced water chestnuts

1 tomato, quartered

1 tablespoon tomato sauce

$1/3$ cup pineapple chunks (optional)

$1/3$ cup shredded carrots (optional)

$1/2$ teaspoon salt

1 cucumber, thinly sliced

Garnish: Green onions, chopped

Chinese parsley, cut into 2-inch lengths

In a wok heat oil on medium heat and cook garlic until light brown. Add onion and stir-fry for 1 minute. Stir in rice, water chestnuts, tomato, tomato sauce, pineapple, carrots and salt; mix well and stir-fry for 3 minutes. Serve with sliced cucumber. Garnish with green onions and Chinese parsley.

MAKES 4 SERVINGS

Fried Rice with Beef

ILLUSTRATED ON PAGE 150

This tasty dish is often served as a snack or can be a meal in itself.

$^1/_2$ pound beef

2 tablespoons vegetable oil

1 clove garlic, finely chopped

1 onion, thinly sliced

1 to 2 eggs, lightly beaten

3 cups cooked rice

1 tomato, quartered

1 tablespoon tomato sauce

$^1/_2$ to 1 tablespoon fish sauce*

1 cucumber, thinly sliced

Garnish: Green onions, chopped

Chinese parsley, cut into 2-inch lengths

Thinly slice beef into 2-inch strips. In a wok heat oil on medium heat and cook garlic until light brown. Stir in beef, onion and eggs. Increase heat to high and stir-fry for 4 to 5 minutes, or until beef is cooked. Add rice, tomato, tomato sauce and fish sauce and stir-fry for 2 minutes. Serve with sliced cucumber. Garnish with green onions and Chinese parsley.

Note: A $^1/_2$ pound of shrimp, pork or chicken can be substituted for the beef.

**The amount of fish sauce used in this recipe depends on the brand selected and personal taste.*

MAKES 6 SERVINGS

Clockwise from left: Fried Rice with Shrimp, Fried Rice with Beef, and Water Chestnut Fried Rice (page 149)

Desserts

Mango with Sticky Rice

ILLUSTRATED ON PAGES 154 AND 155

Fresh ripe mango slices and sticky rice lightly seasoned with coconut milk and sugar is a popular dessert in Thailand and Laos.

3 to 4 ripe mangoes, chilled

3 cups cooked Sticky Rice (recipe page 148)

1 cup coconut milk

2 to 4 tablespoons sugar

$^1/_4$ teaspoon salt

Rinse mangoes and chill them whole. Peel and slice mangoes just before serving to keep the fresh sweet taste. In a saucepan combine sticky rice and coconut milk and cook on medium heat for 5 minutes, or until thick. Stir in sugar and salt. The amount of sugar depends on the sweetness of the mangoes. Reduce heat to low and simmer, covered, for 2 minutes. Serve warm on a platter with chilled mango slices arranged around the edge.

MAKES 4 TO 6 SERVINGS

Mango Bread

Exotic fresh fruit bread of excellent flavor.

3 cups chopped mangoes

$^1/_2$ cup melted butter

3 eggs, lightly beaten

2 tablespoons molasses

$^1/_4$ teaspoon vanilla

3 cups flour

2 teaspoons baking soda

1 tablespoon baking powder

$^1/_2$ teaspoon salt

$^1/_2$ cup shredded coconut

$^1/_4$ cup chopped nuts (optional)

Preheat oven to 350°F. Grease and flour two $3^1/_4$ x 9 x 5-inch loaf pans. In a large mixing bowl combine mangoes, butter, eggs, molasses and vanilla; mix well. Sift together flour, baking soda, baking powder and salt; blend into mango mixture. Lightly stir in coconut and nuts. Pour butter into prepared loaf pans and bake for 1 hour, or until bread tests done.

MAKES 2 LOAVES

Sticky Rice with Banana

ILLUSTRATED ON PAGES 158 AND 159

A tasty dessert of apple banana strips and sticky rice wrapped in banana leaves and steamed. Naturally good!

1 cup coconut milk

3 cups cooked Sticky Rice
   (recipe page 148)

$1/4$ cup palm sugar

$1/8$ teaspoon salt

8 to 10 banana leaves, cut into
   8-inch squares

3 ripe apple bananas, cut into
   1-inch strips

In a saucepan combine coconut milk, sticky rice, palm sugar and salt. Cook on medium heat until thick. Place a layer, about 3 x 3 x $1/2$ inch thick, of the rice mixture in the center of a banana leaf. Place a banana strip on the rice mixture, then wrap it up by lifting up 2 opposite sides of the banana leaf at a time, so the rice goes on top of the banana. Fold under the extra part of the leaf. Place in a steamer and steam for 25 minutes. Serve warm or cold.

MAKES 8 TO 10 SERVINGS

Clockwise from top center: Fried Bananas with Rice Flour (page 161), Sticky Rice with Banana (page 160), Thai Banana Chips (page 161), and Apple Banana with Coconut Milk (page 162)

Fried Bananas with Rice Flour

ILLUSTRATED ON PAGES 158 AND 159

This children's favorite is from bananas coated with shredded coconut and rice flour, then deep-fried. Crisp on the outside, soft and sweet inside.

8 firm ripe bananas	3 tablespoons rice flour
2 eggs, beaten	1 cup shredded coconut
$^1/_4$ cup sugar or honey	$^1/_4$ cup butter

Peel bananas and cut in half lengthwise, then in half crosswise. Combine eggs, sugar and rice flour; mix well. Dip bananas into egg mixture and coat generously. Roll in shredded coconut. Heat butter in a skillet and sauté bananas for 10 minutes, turning once. Serve hot.

MAKES 8 SERVINGS

Thai Banana Chips

ILLUSTRATED ON PAGES 158 AND 159

Easy to make and keeps well for parties and picnics.

6 firm ripe apple bananas

1 cup lime juice

4 cups vegetable oil for deep-frying

1 cup sugar

Peel bananas and slice very thin. Soak banana slices in lime juice for 10 to 15 minutes to prevent them from discoloring; rinse and drain well. Heat oil to 375°F and fry bananas until golden brown and crisp. Drain on absorbent paper. Roll in sugar.

MAKES 3 TO 4 CUPS

Apple Banana with Coconut Milk

ILLUSTRATED ON PAGES 158 AND 159

Apple banana slices cooked in fresh coconut milk is very popular in Thailand.

12 half ripe apple bananas

4 cups fresh coconut milk

$^1/_4$ cup palm sugar

$^1/_8$ teaspoon salt

Peel apple bananas and cut in quarters. Steam for 20 minutes; set aside. In a large pot heat coconut milk, palm sugar and salt on high heat and, as soon as it comes to a boil, add bananas. Reduce heat to a simmer and cook for 1 hour. Serve hot.

MAKES 6 SERVINGS

Golden Threads Dessert

The Thai name for this dessert is "foi tong." It is believed that the recipe came from Portuguese travelers in Thailand a couple of centuries ago. It is a favorite among the children, because it is so sweet.

24 egg yolks (duck eggs preferred)

3 cups water

4 cups sugar

Garnish: Shredded coconut

Require: Golden thread dispenser or an aluminum
cone with a tip opening of $1/32$ inch

In a large bowl beat egg yolks with an electric mixer or wire whip. In a wok bring water and sugar to a boil on high heat and cook until mixture becomes a syrup. Fill golden thread dispenser or aluminum cone with egg yolks, while holding the opening closed. Release opening over the boiling syrup and pipe egg yolks in a circular motion. As soon as the dispenser is empty, scoop up all the cooked yolks and set aside. Refill dispenser and repeat above method until all yolks are used. Chill before serving. To serve, arrange in small individual portions and garnish with shredded coconut.

MAKES 6 TO 8 SERVINGS

Steamed Pumpkin with Custard

Thais are very fond of sweets. This is a very common Thai dessert using pumpkin, squash, young coconut or banana leaves filled with a coconut egg custard. Steam or bake.

3 pumpkins (small enough to fit
 into a steamer)

10 eggs

1 cup coconut milk

$1/2$ cup palm sugar or brown sugar

$1/8$ teaspoon salt

Cut tops off the pumpkins to form a hole 3 inches in diameter. Remove seeds and rinse out pumpkins. Combine eggs, coconut milk, palm sugar and salt; blend well. Fill pumpkins with the egg mixture. Replace tops. Steam for 30 or 45 minutes, or until the egg mixture is of a cooked custard consistency. Chill.

MAKES 4 SERVINGS

Thai Tapioca Pudding

(ILLUSTRATED ON PAGES 164 AND 165)

This is a large pearl tapioca served warm with fresh coconut milk. It differs from American tapioca in that it is more on the liquid side and does not contain milk or eggs.

$1/3$ pound quick-cooking tapioca

3 cups water

3 tablespoons palm sugar or white sugar

$1/8$ teaspoon salt

1 cup coconut milk

Rinse tapioca in cold water; drain and set aside. Bring water to a boil and stir in palm sugar and salt. Add tapioca and return to a boil. Stir in coconut milk. Reduce heat to a simmer. Stir frequently to prevent tapioca from sticking to the bottom of the pan. Cook for 30 minutes. Serve warm or cold.

MAKES 4 TO 6 SERVINGS

Colorful Tapioca

ILLUSTRATED ON PAGES 164 AND 165

Water chestnuts, tapioca flour, and coconut milk make this a very interesting Thai dessert. Since it looks like pomegranate in color, the Thai name for this dessert is "tap-tim-crob," meaning a crispy pomegranate.

$^1/_2$ pound water chesnuts

1 cup tapioca flour

6 cups water

2 cups coconut milk

$^1/_2$ cup sugar or honey

Peel water chestnuts and dice into $^1/_4$-inch cubes. Divide water chestnuts in 4 portions and dye 3 of the portions each a different color. Drain the water chestnuts and toss them in tapioca flour to coat. In a large pot bring water to a boil. Add water chestnuts to the water and bring to a second boil. Drain immediately; then chill in ice cold water. Combine coconut milk and sugar; blend well to dissolve sugar. Chill. Pour over tapioca to serve.

MAKES 4 TO 6 SERVINGS

Beverages

Thai Iced Coffee

$^1/_4$ cup strong French roasted coffee

$^1/_2$ cup boiling water

2 teaspoons sweetened condensed milk

Ice cubes

Combine coffee, boiling water and sweetened condensed milk; stir until blended. Pour into 2 tall glasses filled with ice cubes.

MAKES 2 SERVINGS

Thai Iced Tea

ILLUSTRATED ON OPPOSITE PAGE

$^1/_4$ cup strong Thai tea

$^1/_2$ cup boiling water

2 teaspoons sweetened condensed milk

Ice cubes

Garnish: Mint leaves

Combine tea, boiling water and sweetened condensed milk; stir until blended. Pour into 2 tall glasses filled with ice cubes. Garnish with mint leaves.

MAKES 2 SERVINGS

Guava Daiquiri

2 ounces light rum

2 ounces guava juice concentrate

1 tablespoon fresh lime juice

1 teaspoon sugar

Dash of grenadine

Scoop of cracked ice

Combine rum, guava juice concentrate, lime juice, sugar and grenadine in a blender. Blend on high speed for 30 seconds. Gradually add cracked ice, blending until drink is of a slushy consistency. An excellent before or after dinner drink.

MAKES 2 DRINKS

Lychee Shake

2 scoops lychee sherbet

2 cups milk

Combine lychee sherbet and milk in a blender. Blend on high speed until smooth.

Note: Coconut, mango, banana, guava or lilikoi (passion fruit) sherbet can be substituted for the lychee sherbet.

MAKES 2 SERVINGS

Lilikoi Float

2 scoop lilikoi (passion fruit) sherbet

2 cups chilled lemon-lime soda

In a tall glass combine lilikoi sherbet and lemon-lime soda. Stir with a long spoon until well mixed.

Note: Mango, guava or coconut sherbet can be substituted for the lilikoi sherbet.

MAKES 2 SERVINGS

Evil Princess

An excellent before or after dinner drink. A Keo's original!

2 ounces light rum

2 cups seeded and sliced fresh jackfruits

2 ounces pineapple juice

2 ounces orange juice

1 ounce coconut milk

Scoop of cracked ice

Combine rum, jackfruit, pineapple juice, orange juice and coconut milk in a blender. Blend on high speed for 30 seconds. Gradually add cracked ice, blending until drink is of slushy consistency.

MAKES 2 TO 3 SERVINGS

Mango Daiquiri

ILLUSTRATED ON OPPOSITE PAGE

2 ounces light rum

1 large ripe mango, peeled and seeded

1 tablespoon fresh lemon juice

1 teaspoon sugar (optional)

Scoop of cracked ice

Combine rum, mango, lemon juice and sugar in a blender. Blend on high speed for 30 seconds. Gradually add cracked ice, blending until drink is of a slushy consistency.

MAKES 2 DRINKS

Garnish Ideas and Techniques

Tomato Lotus Flower

Place a tomato stem end down. Starting at the bottom of the tomato make cuts through the skin 1 inch apart, to form petals. In the middle of each petal cut a smaller petal. Slowly peel the outer petal back to form a tomato lotus flower.

Red Chile Flower

Trim off the tip of a red chile pepper. Cut chile pepper lengthwise scissors to form petals. Trim the tip of each petal to a point. Remove seeds. Soak in ice water for 5 minutes, or until red chile flower opens up.

Cucumber Fan

Slice a cucumber in half lengthwise, then cut on the diagonal into sections 2 inches in length. Cut a number of notches along the top of each cucumber section. Make a series of thin cuts down to within $1/2$ inch of the end of each cucumber section. Fan cucumber open by gently pressing down.

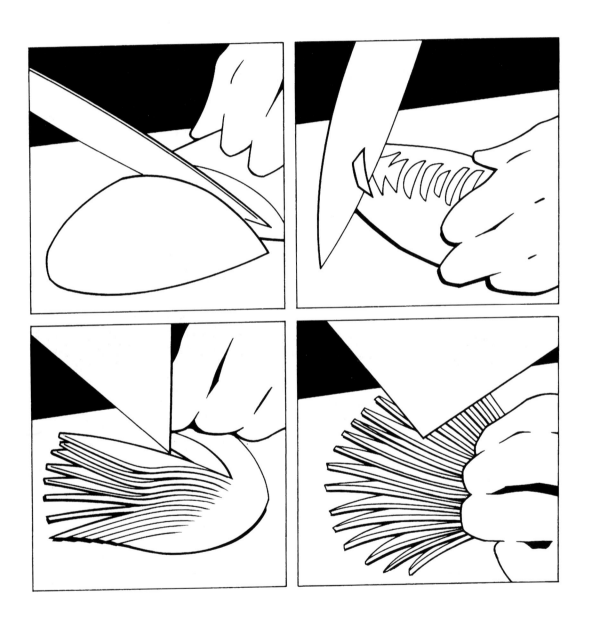

Folded Cucumber

Slice a cucumber in half lengthwise, then cut on the diagonal into sections 1 inch in length. Make 6 thin cuts down to within $1/2$ inch of the opposite side of each cucumber section. Soak in salt water (1 tablespoon salt to 1 quart water) for 15 minutes to make the skin pliable. Tuck under every part until you have 3 folded down.

GARNISH IDEAS AND TECHNIQUES

Cucumber Leaves

Slice off long thick strips from a cucumber. Cut notches on both sides of the strip to resemble a leaf. Etch a thick center vein and thin lines to represent small veins coming out from the center vein. Place cucumber leaves in ice water until ready to use.

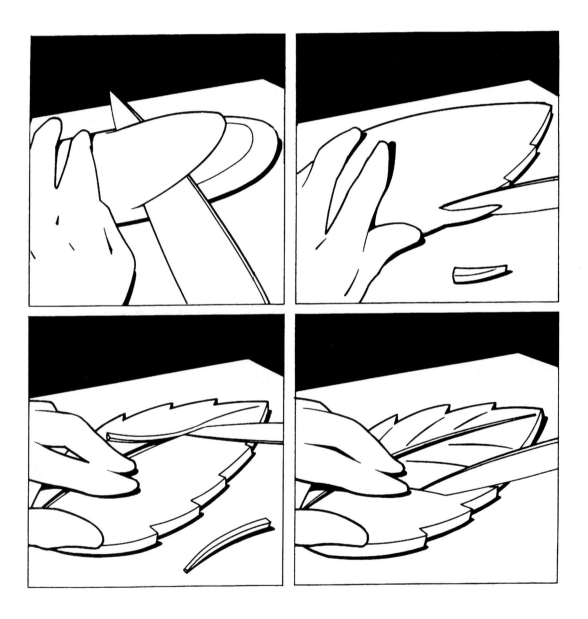

Green Onion Brush

Cut off the root end of a green onion and cut into 2-inch lengths. Insert the point of a needle $1/2$ inch from the end and pull up through the green onion. Repeat this step all the way around the green onion. Soak in ice water for 5 minutes, or until green onion brush curls.

GARNISH IDEAS AND TECHNIQUES

Technique for Wrapping Spring Rolls

Cut rice paper circles into quarters. Place rice paper on a flat surface and brush with water until pliable. Place 2 teaspoons of filling near the edge. Fold rice paper over the filling. Fold the right side over to enclose the filling, then fold over left side. Roll tightly and seal.

Technique for Deboning Chicken Wings

Cut off top portion of chicken wing and reserve for other use. Cut through joint to separate 2 bones. Push meat gently down bones and twist or cut through tendon at base of bones and remove them. Stuff mixture into pocket.

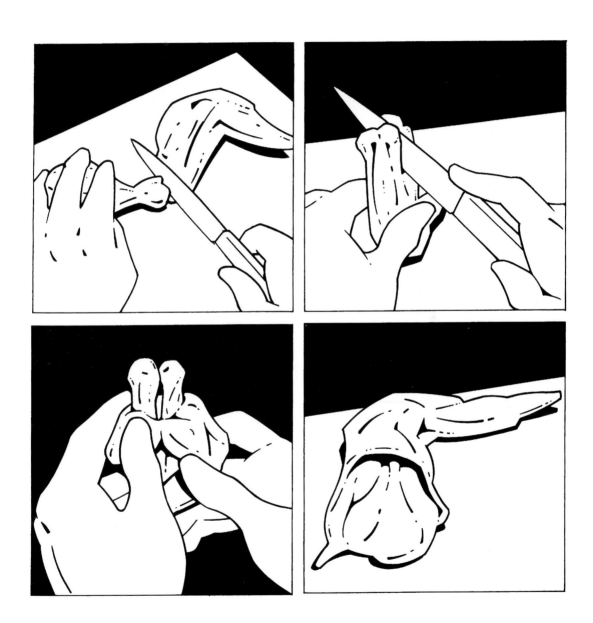

Technique for Cleaning and Scoring Squid

Grasp the squid gently but firmly with both hands and pull the mantle away from the head. Pull the pen (tail skeleton) from the inside of the mantle and discard it. Peel off the thin skin. Rinse the mantle under running cold water and remove the remaining innards. Cut into 2-inch sections. Slit the sections open and lay them on a flat surface. Lightly score the squid on the diagonal in a crosshatch pattern every $^1/_4$ inch.

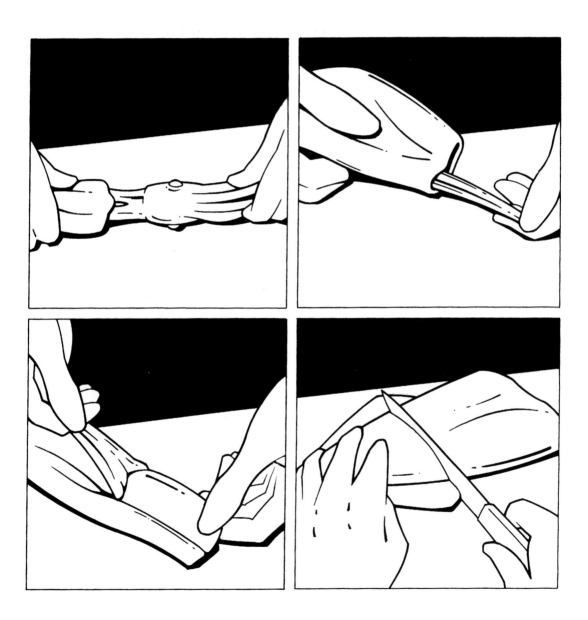

Thai Eating Habits

Chopsticks are used only when noodles are served in Thai homes or restaurants. Most Thais eat with a fork and a spoon. The spoon held in the right hand carries the food while the fork is held in the left hand and is used to push food onto the spoon. In the villages or on informal occasions the spoon and fingers are acceptable, especially when sticky rice is served. The meals are served family style, which allows you to taste everything served on the table.

Thais enjoy eating and drinking. When not eating, it is normal to discuss plans for the next meal. There are no restrictions on food or beverage in Thailand. Buddhist restrictions on taking life do not prevent Thais from eating meat and even the monks and nuns eat meat when they are served by the people.

There are food vendors everywhere in Thailand selling little snacks or full meal menus. The English version of Thai menus in most restaurants in Thailand may be a bit strange for foreigners, such items as Lady's Fingers Salad, Cow Pad, Horse's Urine Eggs, Mouse's Droppings Chile, Metallic Manures Soup. It is perfectly okay to ask about items unfamiliar or to refuse something which is served to you when you are a guest in Thailand.

Menu Suggestions

FOR 2
Crisp Fried Tofu
Green Papaya Salad
Satay Shrimp
Water Chestnut Fried Rice

FOR 4
Fish Patties
Spicy Shrimp Soup with Lemongrass
Thai Beef Salad
Cashew Chicken
Green Shrimp Curry
Steamed Rice
Tapioca Pudding

FOR 6
Crisp Noodles
Thai Ginger Chicken Soup
Calamari Salad with Fresh Lemongrass
Thai Shrimp with Garlic
Beef with Fresh Sweet Basil
Panang Duck
Brown Rice
Mango with Sticky Rice

FOR 8
Keo's Thai Spring Rolls
Spicy Shrimp Soup with Lemongrass
Chieng Mai Chicken Salad
Whole Fish with Fresh Ginger and Yellow Bean Sauce
Beef with Oyster Sauce
Evil Jungle Prince with Mixed Vegetables
Sticky Rice
Brown Rice
Apple Banana with Coconut Milk

Index

KEO'S THAI CUISINE